IN THE PRISON
OF HIS DAYS

IN THE PRISON
OF HIS DAYS

THE LILLIPUT PRESS
1988

First published in 1988 by
THE LILLIPUT PRESS LTD
Gigginstown, Mullingar,
Co. Westmeath, Ireland

British Library Cataloguing in Publication Data

In the prison of his days: a miscellany for
Nelson Mandela on his 70th birthday.
1. Literature, to 1982.   Special subjects:
Humanism-Anthologies
I. McCormack, W. J. (William John), *1947-*
808.8'0384

ISBN 0 946640 33 5

Acknowledgments

The editor and publisher gratefully acknowledge permission to publish the
contents of *In the Prison of His Days*. In addition to the individual authors, the
following should also be noted: 'Sri Lanka' by Richard Murphy is published by
permission of *The New York Review of Books*; 'Als Schriftsteller immer auch
Zeitgenosse' by Gunter Grass is published in English translation by permission of
the author and Luchterhand Literaturverlag (Darmstadt); Wally Serote's interview is published by permission of *Index on Censorship*, where it first appeared
in the issue of May 1988. The editor is grateful for the advice of Dennis Tate in
relation to some technical aspects of the publication, also Kader and Louise
Asmal, and the much-put-upon translators in Derry.

Cover design by The Graphionies
Typeset by Redsetter Ltd of Dublin
Printed by Billings & Sons Ltd of Worcester, England

Contents

EDITORIAL
Intellectual Responsibility

The miscellany of writings which follows has been brought together
to mark Nelson Mandela's seventieth birthday. Given that prison
walls have surrounded him in his seventieth year, as in his fiftieth,
and given his illness later in the year, no easy celebration could be
indulged. To acknowledge the special and difficult circumstances of
the occasion, the format of a special issue of a magazine has been
adopted. Beginning with an editorial, it includes poems interspersed
between fiction and commentary; a moving interview with an ex-
prisoner and poet is accompanied by essays in scholarly criticism.
Most of the contributors are Irish, because the idea for the book
originated with the Irish Anti-Apartheid Movement. But as generous
evidence of Mandela's unique appeal to the world at large, we also
have very distinguished contributions from England, France,
Germany, Hungary, Nigeria, the Soviet Union, and South Africa
itself. A theme, the writer's responsibility in a world of increasing
domination and terror, runs through the miscellany.

This theme, as Chinua Achebe so ably demonstrates, provides
even an opportunity for celebration of a kind. The traditional art
form (or art practice) of *mbari* which he describes has provided a
model for the merging of different tones and perspectives; *mbari*
allows for the commemoration of life in all its aspects, 'its good
points and its problems'. With this kind of precedent, the miscellany
has been able to mark Nelson Mandela's long years of imprisonment
in a manner which accommodates the directness of Edward Bond
alongside the seeming absurd humour of Daniil Kharms – arrest,
detention, brutality are their implicit points of convergence.

Among the Irish contributors, there is a high concentration on the
Southern states of the USA (in Hubert Butler, Desmond Hogan,
Benedict Kiely, even Michael Longley in the last of the three poems
included here) as if Mandela's plight could be sensitively approached
through a region which is more familiar and which nonetheless has in
the recent past known dreadful racial prejudice. It is hoped that all of
these essays and poems – the unmistakable tones of Ben Kiely
modulating effortlessly (yet with feeling) from the names of Irish
friends to the fathomless vacuity of James Earl Ray's crime and
punishment, the suavity of John Banville, the striking honesty of
Wally Serote in interview – will each serve to illuminate the central

theme.

A writer's notion of honesty, his sustained and demanding negotiations between the world and the word, constitutes a topic of great controversy in the late twentieth century. Intellectual responsibility in the political domain is now a subject of acute concern in the United States, the Middle East, Europe, and the Third World. No political crisis since the end of the Second World War has made a more powerful and eloquent demand on the writer's attention than that fomented by the increasingly violent apartheid regime of South Africa. Many have declined to respond. We are tempted at times to quote W. H. Auden:

> Intellectual disgrace
> Stares from every human face.

The poem from which these lines are taken, 'In Memory of W. B. Yeats', was written on the eve of the War, at the end of what Auden elsewhere called 'a low dishonest decade'. But, in practice, not *all* writers and intellectuals have declined *all* challenges. For example, Samuel Beckett's translation of the Surrealist declaration of 1934 is only one of several pieces on the topic which he rendered into English for Nancy Cunard's massive *Negro Anthology*. The recovery of this piece should prompt a reconsideration of the precise political milieu which Beckett encountered when he began what has turned out to be a life-time's sojourn in France. It is here reproduced in this homage to Nelson Mandela by the translator's express permission.

All the contributors bring a sample of their work as homage to a truly great man. (In the case of Kharms, the active contributor is of course the translator; in the case of Austin Clarke, it is to his son Dardis to whom we are immediately grateful.) Most of the work does not impinge directly on the state of South Africa, and yet the writings gathered here show how Irish writers and others have responded to the challenge of racism. This little anthology calls for unflinching attention to the moral scandal symbolised in Nelson Mandela's life imprisonment. It offers no bouquet of verbal tributes and few felicitations, because only those who are prepared to think astringently can presume to advise, as Auden, did:

> In the prison of his days
> Teach the free man how to praise.

Nelson Mandela is such a man. Greetings and praise will be fully appropriate only on the day of South African liberation. Then we will build a new *mbari* together.

W. J. Mc Cormack — *October 1988*

MARY BENSON

On Behalf of Nelson Mandela

In Dublin's Merrion Square a sculpture honours the most famous
political prisoner of our time, Nelson Mandela. Ireland's gesture
expresses the extraordinary, the historic impact which the life of a
man incarcerated in remote South Africa has had on the international
community. And this book is but one of innumerable tributes in
celebration of Mandela's birthday on 18 July 1988. Mandela would
not want to be singled out, but during more than a quarter of a
century in jail he has become a symbol of South Africa's uniquely
oppressed society and the embodiment of his people's prolonged
struggle to be free.

The South African government hoped it had crushed that struggle
by sentencing Mandela and other leaders to life imprisonment and by
outlawing their organisation, the African National Congress. Yet
today the ANC (founded in 1912) is acknowledged as the most
powerful force fighting apartheid. It has done so through years of
bitter unrest and ever more savage states of emergency. And despite
the banning of books about Mandela – it is even illegal to quote him
or to display his portrait – young South Africans born long after he
disappeared behind prison walls regard him as their authentic leader.
His almost legendary reputation has been enhanced by reports from
men who have served alongside him on Robben Island and from the
foreign visitors rarely permitted to see him.

Born into the royal family of the Tembu people in the Transkei,
Mandela was brought up with a sense of responsibility. But he had a
taste for adventure, and his Xhosa name (Rolihlahla) appropriately
means 'stirring up trouble'. (It was an English woman teacher who,
recoiling at the Xhosa, called him Nelson.) To close friends, he is
Madiba, his clan name.) After a college education cut short by a
students' strike, he turned his back on the prospect of chieftainship
and escaped to the thrusting city of Johannesburg, where he found
himself among thousands forced to live in 'locations' or shanty towns
and subjected to continual harassment from police under the hated
pass laws.

His political education had begun and, encouraged by a new

friend Walter Sisulu, he joined the ANC. With Oliver Tambo they formed a remarkable team. (Sisulu was to remain at Mandela's side through much of their imprisonment while Tambo was to lead the struggle from exile.) Joining other young African nationalists, they formed a Youth League to galvanise the somewhat conservative ANC. They sustained a policy of non-violence even in confronting the intensifying violence of the immensely powerful Afrikaner state. When 8,500 men and women – most of them African but with significant Indian support, and a handful of white volunteers – courted imprisonment, Mandela, learning to control his own hot temper, was appointed Volunteer-in-Chief of the Defiance Campaign.

Among organisers given a suspended sentence Mandela, like other leaders, was repeatedly banned from political activity. But he had meanwhile qualified as an attorney and established a partnership with Tambo. If they had not already been rebels against apartheid, said Tambo, their experiences as lawyers would have remedied that deficiency. Every case, every visit to the prisons, reminded them of the suffering and humiliation burning into their people. The laws, Mandela said, were immoral, unjust and intolerable.

In December 1956, one hundred and fifty-six men and women of all races were arrested and charged with treason. Mandela, among thirty defendants still on trial after four and a half years, played an important part in destroying the state's case. All the accused were found not guilty.

On 21 March 1960 police violence was exposed more shockingly than ever before when they shot dead sixty-nine men, women and children at a township named Sharpeville. At this crucial time Mandela was deputed to lead the struggle from underground. It meant sacrificing his professional life but, far more painfully, his family life also: in 1958 he had married Winnie Nomzamo Madikizela, a lovely young medical social worker, and they had two small daughters. With Sisulu he organised one last non-violent strike, and as he daringly eluded the police the press dubbed him the Black Pimpernel. Defying the biggest call up of police and military since the Second World War, tens of thousands of workers responded to the call to stay at home. It was not enough. In a secret meeting with foreign correspondents, Mandela gravely declared, 'If the government reaction is to crush by naked force our non-violent struggle, we will have to reconsider our tactics. In my mind we are closing a chapter on this question of a non-violent policy.' Seven months later in December 1961 that chapter was ritually closed when the President General of the ANC, Chief Albert Lutuli, was awarded the Nobel Peace Prize in recognition, so he said, of the organisation's long history of non-violence. During the following week in South Africa sabotage against symbols of apartheid marked the birth of Umkhonto we Sizwe (Spear of the Nation). Leaflets proclaimed, 'The time comes in the life of any nation when there only remain two choices: submit or fight. That time has now come to South Africa. We shall not submit . . . .' While the sabotage continued Mandela made an exhilirating tour of African states to win support for the ANC. After a visit to London and a brief course of military training in Algeria, he slipped back into South Africa.

On 5 August 1962 he was captured and sentenced to five years for 'inciting' workers to strike and for leaving the country without valid travel documents. Within months he was again in the dock as Accused Number One, alongside Walter Sisulu and others, in the Rivonia Trial, charged with attempting to overthrow the government. Mandela did not deny planning sabotage. 'I did not plan it . . . because I have any love of violence,' he declared. 'I planned it as a result of a calm and sober assessment of the political situation that had arisen after many years of tyranny, exploitation and oppression of my people by the whites.'

His statement from the dock has moved people in many lands with its final affirmation: 'I have fought against white domination and I have fought against black domination. I have cherished the ideal of a democratic and free society in which all persons live together in harmony and with equal opportunities. It is an ideal which I hope to live for and to achieve. But if needs be, it is an ideal for which I am prepared to die.'

On 12 June 1964 Mandela, Sisulu, Ahmed Kathrada, Govan Mbeki, Raymond Mhlaba, Andrew Mlangeni, Elias Motsoaledi and Dennis Goldberg were sentenced to life imprisonment. Mandela and the other black defendants were flown to Robben Island, a rocky outcrop surrounded by forbidding seas, some seven miles off Cape Town. There they were held with a score of other politicals in a special section of individual cells. They slept on thin mats, washed in cold water; the food was inedible, the warders abusive. Newspapers were forbidden. Every six months they were allowed one visit of half an hour and one letter of five hundred words, censored. These men, whom the *New York Times* said were regarded as heroes, the George Washingtons and Benjamin Franklins of South Africa, laboured with pick-axes and spades in a lime quarry, year after year, through cold year after year, through cold dank winters and baking summers.

From the start they had decided that no matter what they were subjected to, no weakness would be shown. Fellow prisoners came to regard Mandela and Sisulu with a kind of reverence. 'Mandela taught me how to survive,' one was to say. 'When I was ill he could have asked anybody else to see to me. He came to me personally. He even cleaned my toilet.'

Studies became a lifeline and each man shared his special knowledge of politics and law, economics, literature, and languages. Their protests (in which Mandela confronted prison officials with firm authority), their hunger strikes and go-slows, together with protests from the outside world, gradually won improvements such as beds, warmer clothing and more vegetables until by the 1970s visits had been increased and labour in the quarry was replaced by seaweed collecting or road building. In time, hard labour was ended altogether and, finally, the prisoners were allowed newspapers.

On an unforgettable occasion the boilers broke down, there was no food, and the men were kept locked in their cells. After furious protests food was eventually brought into their yard late at night. But when they entered the yard, hunger was forgotten as they gazed up, for the first time in years seeing the night sky, the Milky Way, the Southern Cross, all of them marvelling.

Throughout the nineteen years Mandela spent on Robben Island, Winnie had endured increasingly harsh restrictions as she struggled to make a living and bring up her daughters. Imprisoned in solitary confinement in 1969, she was twice brought to trial under the Terrorism Act and, each time, was acquitted. Clearly an inspiration to young blacks in Soweto, she was again detained after their uprising in 1976 and was released only to be banished to a hostile village in an Afrikaner backwater. A one-woman resistance movement, she eventually emerged triumphant, unbanned and back home in Soweto. In 1982 Mandela, Sisulu and three of the other Rivonia men were suddenly transferred to Pollsmoor Maximum Security Prison on the mainland. Two years later a remarkable event occurred:

contact visits were permitted. For the first time in twenty-two years Mandela was permitted to embrace his wife.

After three meetings with him during 1986 the Commonwealth Group of Eminent Persons reported, 'We found him unmarked by any trace of bitterness despite his long imprisonment. His overriding concern was for the welfare of all races in South Africa in a just society; he longed to be allowed to contribute to the process of reconciliation.'

In South Africa rigid censorship under prolonged states of emergency has failed to conceal escalating brutality. State violence hugely exceeds Umkhonto's: hundreds of children have been killed by the state and of 30,000 detainess held since 1986 it is estimated that a third have been children, many of whom have been tortured. At least a thousand detainees are still held. Community leaders are assassinated, and conditions have been deliberately created for so-called black on black violence.

Meanwhile throughout the world the demand intensifies: Free Mandela! It is he who holds the key to South Africa's future. What an appalling, tragic waste – for whites as well as for blacks – that his wisdom and strength, his great generosity and humour, have not been used in bring sanity to that country. When State President Botha announced in January 1983 that Nelson Mandela might be freed if he renounced violence, Mandela's reply was uncompromising, 'Let *him* renounce violence. Let him say that he will dismantle apartheid.' Addressing the people, Mandela declared, 'I cherish my own freedom dearly but I care even more for your freedom.' And he concluded, 'I cannot and will not give any undertaking at a time when I and you, my people, are not free. Your freedom and mine cannot be separated. I will return.'

CHINUA ACHEBE

Literature as Celebration: An Address
(*to the International Writers Conference, Dublin, June 1988*).

What does it mean to be given the last word in this extraordinary congress of highly articulate and diverse exponents of the literary arts? Am I expected to attempt a summary? Well, I couldn't, even if I wished to. There has been so much and I am quite sure that I have not understood all of it perfectly. In any event there are good reasons for me to leave what has been said where it has been said and strike out, as it were, on my own. The main reason for this is that I belong to a tradition which is not well represented here, though I do admit I did hear echoes of affinity now and again.

Many years ago at a literary conference in Stockholm, a Swedish author and journalist said to visiting African writers words to this effect, 'You fellows are lucky. Your governments put you in prison. In Sweden nobody pays any attention to us, no matter what we write.' Well, we apologised profusely to him for what had suddenly emerged as an unfair advantage.

As these marvellous days in Dublin draw to a close, I cannot help thinking of that poor Swede and of the problematic relationship between the Poet and the Emperor which was implied in his lament. It occurs to me that, if the Emperor were around here this week, he would be very happy with us because we would not seem to him a likely bunch to upset his kingdom. He would certainly approve of a clear division of labour in which poets wrote poetry, and he ruled his empire in peace, which seems to be the ardent desire of many poets at this conference.

Let me tell you briefly about the rather different perceptions that underlie my own practice. Some of these perceptions come from social/historical sources; which is not to deny the presence also of a very strong, personal, individual element. And I had better make it clear at the outset that I am not trying to convert anybody to my way of thinking. I don't believe in conversions and missionaries. Anyone can tell me from the bowels of Christ (or even from more salubrious surroundings) that I may be mistaken. And it won't be the first time I've heard that, nor difficult for me to accept.

Although' *The Irish Times* of yesterday called me the 'man who invented African Literature' I must say to you and to the hearing of the gods that I never make such claims myself, for I know that they (the gods, I mean) waste no time at all in finishing off anyone who presumes to lay a proprietary hand to even the least object in the vast display of *mbari* art.

Mbari is a celebration of art which was demanded of the community from time to time by its presiding divinity – generally the Earth goddess, Ala, who (by the way) is both the goddess of creativity and the custodian of social morality. *Mbari* is a celebration of the world, in its immense and diverse wholeness, in sculpture and wall painting. Every significant encounter which man makes in his journey through life – especially every new, unaccustomed and thus threatening encounter – is quickly recognised and assigned a place in this always renewed, always expanding creative panorama.

For example, when Europe made its appearance in Igbo society in the alarming person of the District Officer, he was immediately given a seat among the customary images of beasts and humans and gods. To the Igbo mentality art must, among other uses, provide safety like the lightning conductor which arrests the explosion of destructive electrical potentials and channels them harmlessly to earth. The Igbo insist that any presence which is ignored, which is shut out, which is denied celebration, becomes a focus for anxiety and disruption.

But the celebration of *mbari* was not blind adulation. The white District Officer was obviously not a matter for joy, nor the man with the marks of small-pox on his body, nor the woman copulating with a dog. So *mbari* did not celebrate a perfect world but the world the community knew in reality as well as imagination, with all its good points and its problems.

Even if I spoke about *mbari* for the rest of the time allotted to me I could not tell you all the important statements it sought to make on the relationships of art and its makers to the general community. But let me mention two very briefly: (a) the creators of the images were not artists as such but ordinary men and women chosen to work in seclusion with master artists; (b) after the completion of the work and the celebration by the community, the *mbari* building and its vast treasure of art is abandoned to ruin and decay. Years later the goddess would demand another celebration and the process of building a new *mbari* would be repeated, by other members of the village.

I offer this as one illustration of my pre-colonial inheritance of traditional art as celebration of my reality; of art in its social dimension; of the creative potential in all of us, and of the need to exercise this potential again and again. Now I must speak briefly about the literature which I received in the colonial package. It was a strange inheritance, but an inheritance it was all the same. Unlike my other legacy this one had no intention to celebrate my world. On the contrary it was a *heritage of denigration*. And really this is not to be wondered at.

Colonisation is a very complex affair. You do not walk in, seize the land, the person, the history of another and then sit back and compose panegyrics to him. If you did you would be convicting yourself of banditry. So, instead, you construct very elaborate excuses. The man is unfit to run himself and his affairs. Perhaps the man does not even own these things you are carting off; they just happen to be lying around where he is. Finally, the man cannot be, like you, fully human.

In the 1870s Durham University arranged an affiliation with Fourah Bay College in Sierra Leone. An editorial in the London *Times* wondered whether Durham would affiliate next with the zoo. The matter was as serious as that! Much later the great Albert Schweitzer, philosopher, theologian, missionary, doctor, humanitarian, would concede African humanity – conditionally. The black man is my brother but my junior brother. In between the *Times* editorial and the Schweitzer confession, a lot of literature was made, most of it entirely predictable in its offensiveness! But a few 'serious' writers also contributed to this colonial genre, among them Joseph Conrad and an Irishman who had served the empire as a District Officer in Nigeria – Joyce Cary.

The key issue in the literature of denigration is the inferiority of the colonised. One of the characters in John Buchan's famous colonial novel, *Prester John*, says this 'is the difference between white and black, the gift of responsibility. . . . As long as we know and practise it we will rule not in Africa alone but wherever there are dark men who live only for their bellies.' But the absence of the gift of responsibility in the colonised native is nothing compared to the absence in him of the gift of human speech. This goes all the way back to the dawn of the age of colonisation, to Shakespeare's Caliban ('slave . . . savage') who knew not his own meaning but 'wouldst gabble like a thing most brutish.' But Shakespeare allowed his Caliban to learn and to speak great poetry in the end.

Conrad peopled or packed his Africa with Calibans who made 'violent babble of uncouth sounds' and 'exchanged short grunting phrases' even amongst themselves and to the bitter end. In the entire novel, *Heart of Darkness*, Conrad allows no more than a dozen words to one and a half Africans: the cannibal (Caliban) who says, 'Catch 'im . . . eat 'im', and the half-caste who announces 'Mista Kurtz – he dead.'

When Wolé Soyinka made his highly advertised attempt to dismiss the négritude movement with the clever quip that a tiger does not talk tigritude, Senghor – one of the founders of the movement – made an adequate reply, namely: *but the tiger does not talk*. It not only answered Soyinka, it put forward a concise manifesto for African literature. *The Negro talks*. And talking is a measure of that humanity which colonialism sought to deny. This is what African literature celebrates today. It restores the tradition of *mbari* and it challenges the images of denigration and dehumanisation.

Needless to say it could not possibly accept some of the constraints one has heard proposed here this week that poetry must be private, must be introspective and lyrical. Of course poetry can be all of that. But if it chooses, and if it can challenge itself to it, it can also be communal, even activist. And I am not talking about propaganda. I am talking about poetry.

Agostinho Neto was a doctor in a poor suburb of Luanda in colonial Angola. He wrote very delicate poetry in his spare time. One day after witnessing a particularly brutal action of the Portuguese colonial regime, he wrote a poem addressed to his mother in which he said:

I wait no more
I am the awaited

He shut down his surgery and went into the bush. As the guerrillas of the MPLA fought against the Portuguese they recited lines from his poetry.

Such things are possible.

MICHAEL LONGLEY

The Man of Two Sorrows

Since the day after he was conceived his father
Was killed, he will become The Man of Two Sorrows
Whose mother is wading into the river to delay
His birth, squatting all night on a stepping stone
That flattens his head, headstone pressing fontanel,
Waters breaking under water that nearly drowns him,
Until the morning when he is born and she dies
And the drops of first milk vanish in the river.

The King of the Island

The man who owns it calls himself the king
Of this windy island: these are his waters
The gannet penetrates without a splash, turning
On the bright sixpence I toss there for luck.

It is like a marriage when we ring the birds
Whose heavy wingbeats we gather from the air,
Whose wrists we encircle with a long number
The king of the island will read when he returns.

The Shack

I lie awake between the two sleeping couples.
Their careful breathing in the Blue Ridge Mountains
Disturbs me more than the engine ticking over
At the end of the lane, the repetitive whippoorwill,
The downpour's crescendo on corrugated iron.
Though there are doors between them and me, perhaps
They will risk making love like embarrassed parents
While I remain motionless on my creaking divan.
They have shown me a copperhead, indian fire, pinks
And buzzards like mobiles where the storm clouds hang.
I might as well be outside in the steamy field
Interrupting again the opossums' courtship,
Paralysing with torchlight pink noses, naked tails
Just beyond the shithouse where, like a fall of snow,
The equalising lime has covered our excrement.
Tomorrow when we pass the Pentecostal church
The wayside pulpit will read 'Thanks, Lord, for the rain.'

GUNTER GRASS

The Writer, Always a Man of His Time
(read at the International PEN Congress in Hamburg, May 1986:
translated from German by Aoibheann Mullan and Kevin O'Donnell)

The reflection of contemporary events in the literature of any era presupposes the existence of writers who see themselves as actively involved in it, for whom even the most trivial political events are not some extra-aesthetic distraction but the actual basis of their resistance. Such writers have no desire to be assimilated into timelessness with every word they write, nor do they try to compensate for lack of distance from the events of the moment with narrative inspiration. As conscious opponents of academic notions of fine-ground poetics they have been under attack for as long as literature has existed, whether by the state or by Inquisitors, who even today, in the guise of literary pundits, revel in their censoriousness.

However, I don't want to get lost among fixed terms like 'ivory tower' or 'littérature engagé', but rather I want to report on my experiences as a writer and a reader, experiences which have never been free of contemporary pressure and political interference. Even in my excuses and games of hide and seek, I was always a committed contemporary, a combination of roles to which not only writers in German are condemned. The Spanish Civil War provides exemplary instances.

Fifty years ago, in the course of the Spanish Civil War, the Second World war was being prepared. All the ideologies which have since prevailed or are again latent had been set in place, with the result that the bourgeois democrats coyly accepted the falangist putsch out of fear of the communists, while the left was further weakened by the Stalinist terror, to the detriment of the Spanish Republic. It remains an unresolved dispute, and at the same time a suppressed one, for all that the literature of the period presented a many sided image of the degeneration of the substance of anti-fascist influence and hinted at imminent betrayal through the Stalin-Hitler pact. From Neruda and Hemingway, through Orwell, Malraux and Bernanos, to Koestler, Renn, Kisch and Regler, writers from all over the world were present as eye-witnesses, were in their books more clear sighted than the politicians of the 1930s. Their collective testimony remains a reproach to us.

From Gustav Regler's book *Das Ohr des Malchus* [Malchus's Ear], I quote a scene in which a scattered group from the International Brigade barely escapes liquidation by a communist unit under the notorious André Marty:

> 'I didn't want to believe it at first,' said a young Jewish boy who had previously been in my communications unit.
>
> 'But then he started to curse like a nutter. Nothing but bellyaching about Trots and counter-revolutionaries. Well, we knew then what the score was!'
>
> He scratched his head.
>
> 'But he aimed to miss us by a hairsbreadth.'
>
> 'Why didn't he shoot us?' asked the one from my former communications corps.
>
> 'Because he's a coward, because he knew he'd snuff it. Hangmen are always cowards. It's a coward's job. Adolf is a coward and Stalin no less so.'

Crude prose, as if it had been taken down on the spot. There was little time for art. Brought inexorably close to fascist and Stalinist terror, the lack of distance had to be replaced by moments precisely captured. Orwell's *Homage to Catalonia* is similarly subject to the constraints of this stylistic necessity and it remains just as valid today. Without the prior experience of the Spanish Civil War, his later, more detached allegorical books would not have had the impact which makes them controversial, if not prohibited, even today.

To trace the biography of every writer from just the German speaking world who was in Spain would require an entire chapter. Each case would show the risks that writers run when they confront their own age – all forced into exile, some into death, many subsequently into conformity or silence, others into expulsion as renegades, their books fed to Oblivion's devouring wolf. And yet without them we would know only the side of history concerned with political power-shifts, military victories, treaties and the breaking of treaties, statistics and official government documents. Such a historiography passes over the head of the individual in the mass of sufferers. It tidies up what until the day before yesterday lay in a chaotic heap. The view from below is omitted. As a rule underdogs leave behind very few documents. The historian becomes aware of these gaps only if writers make themselves conspicuous by speaking out, writers who didn't withdraw into subjectivity during the bad times in order to survive, understandable though that would have been. Instead they remained exposed. They watched, stored up, and observed their own day; more or less involved, more or less damaged by their experiences.

Is the writer then, as a sideline, to be made to serve as a stop-gap for official history? He fills out what is missed in the historical process by all the large-scale studies. Grimmelshausen's *Simplizissimus* [Simpleman] could be read as a gloss on the Thirty Years' War; you could write off Babel's *Red Cavalry*, Celine's *Journey to the End of Night*, and Remarque's *All Quiet on the Western Front* as performing a similar service. Now and again, in footnotes and in references, historians call upon literature as supplementary evidence worthy of mention.

But in doing so they prefer to overlook the fact that the writer, as a perceptive man of his times, does not so much give order to the course of history as preserve its absurdity, by burying the big dates under a thousand small ones, bringing the underdog into view by changing the perspective and speaking up on behalf of fear, distress, even cowardice, and thus reducing so-called heroes to human dimensions and turning history on its head. Great political events and decisive battles aren't really his raw material. For him what counts much more is everyday life under the control of prevailing opinion; this he uncovers layer by layer and gives it a voice.

I will mention three authors, three book titles, I feel close to, that exemplify for me this kind of writer and literature, and whose lasting influence derives not least from contemporary reference: Dos Passos, Carlo Emilio Gadda, Alfred Döblin, and their three city novels, *Manhattan Transfer*, *That Awful Mess on Via Merulana*, and *Berlin Alexanderplatz*.

All three write in emulation of James Joyce, without making a Nothing-which-Nothings out of the creator of modern epic, and without displaying a trace of Epigone's Dependency. They create literary reality from the functioning chaos of metropolitan grids and stratifications. Their heroes are on the losing side, whose downfall is preordained. All comes to nothing: ex-prisoner Franz Biberkopf can't make a go of his new life despite repeated efforts; nor can Rome's Commissioner Ingravallo solve the robbery and murder in the Via Merulana; likewise the dishwashers' dream of the dishwasher, rising to wealth and power, the American Dream – all comes to nothing. Yet embedded in the commonplace, under a landslide of obsessively recorded facts, hidden in sub-plot and digression, swaddled in puns, or blatantly introduced by way of quotations, there is present in all three books, alongside mythical eruption, a history of the now. Now the end of the twenties and the collapse of the Weimar Republic, now Dollar Hubris anticipating the great depression, now to end the list the banality of early Italian fascism. Since their lives are determined not by the ruling powers but by private despair, political events are the mere inner lining of all that happens. Here the outer surface still holds, there the seams are already beginning to burst. Or to put the argument the other way round: the claim to power of the prevailing political system, whatever it is, its desire to colonise every aspect of life, even dreams, this familiar voracity has to recognise its limits and be excluded, because the obsessions of the disintegrating tragi-comic hero happen to be stronger.

Franz Biberkopf, the transport worker, who in-between times sells newspapers at the Alexanderplatz, advises an old man who wants to get into the business:

> You've got to have connections and a good stand. When it rains, it's wet. For business to be good you must have prize fights and changes in the government. At Ebert's death, they tell me, people simply grabbed the papers away from you.

Döblin, Dos Passos, Gadda: these three are exemplary writers for the twenties. The barbarism to come is germinating in their epic material mass, but they don't at the same time spout prophecy over the reader's head, they don't even openly agitate, for there has always been another literature related to the present based on the agitprop model: books, poems, plays advocating direct action, whether focussed explicitly on the left or the right, conveying nothing but their immediate message. Bound to certain historical periods, characterised by their pathos and enthusiasm, they are only interesting as documents of ideological pulp literature comparable to the tracts of cantankerous clerics. They cannot live up to their claim of being a literary mirror of their respective eras.

The much-quoted 'hero' was saddled with the burden of dogmatic ideology and became a caricature of itself. Just as the demand for socialist realism appears at best amusing, even though the longing for the heroic and the demand for the positive are again booming. Is this to boost American self-confidence or is a miserable attempt to win the Vietnam War by means of a literary late tackle or re-run of its events?

The writer as a man of his times in the sense which I mean will always move out of step with the spirit of his time. As an example and in remembrance, I single out Uwe Johnson whose work from the early novels to the four volumes of the *Anniversaries* [two edited volumes in English] bears witness to his and our time. Intent on every detail, almost in the manner of a book-keeper, and setting himself the most stringent literary standards, he has chronicled, almost as an aside, the story of the genesis of the German Democratic Republic, the transition (now smooth, now abrupt) from National Socialism to Stalinism, admittedly so relentlessly that his books are not officially available in the state where they originated; one more German writer who, for political reasons, cannot be made accessible.

And what makes his books ostensibly so dangerous, what earns them the dubious honour of being banned? I select one example in hundreds from the fourth volume of the *Anniversaries*. Due to insufficient willingness to display the opportunism rife among his countrymen, the teacher Kliefoth comes to grief when, in the autumn of '49, a new National Anthem is to be introduced:

Anxious to show off a musical expertise they don't have, people like Frau Lindsetter say loudly that Kliefoth has tripped up over the issue of the anthem. For what every state needs, its anthem, was integrated into the timetable of the Fritz Reuter High School that November. In two-four time, with three simple, symmetrical sections, it danced attention on the rhymed intention of a collective Subject – a

Having Risen From the Ru-ins
To Face the Future And to Serve

Thee – *Deutschland einig Vaterland* – and to serve it well so that (the finale) the sun would shine on this our land more beautifully than never before.

With an irony which examines the subject from every angle, Johnson exposes the 'pompous piece' and divulges that the melody is a plagiarism from a film number of 1936 'Wasser für Canitoga' (Water for Canitoga) with Hans Albers as the original vocalist.

For souls loyal to the state, it could be distressing to read how Johnson proves his case line by line and to top it all reveals within his narrative framework the extent to which the foundation of the First German Farmers' and Workers' State was a sham and a confidence trick. Besides Kliefoth, the music teacher Buck is destroyed by this affair: one retires, the other goes to the west where the other German state is seen to base its legitimacy on different plagiarisms.

Uwe Johnson's review of the early 1950s, in which no detail is regarded as insignificant, shows that the constitutents of that era remain unchanged today. This is brought home to the reader through the narrative framework of the *Anniversaries*. The New York setting, and the daily *New York Times*, reveal the dominant events of the day, the Vietnam War and the daily more threatening imminent invasion of Czechoslovakia by the armies of the Warsaw Pact.

This extraordinary literary endeavour – an ocean of words between Manhattan and Mecklenburg – this imposition on the reader which shuns no digression, this epoch-making achievement continues to be ignored, for all the respectful mumbling that goes on, ignored in the east in silence and in the west behind literary chit-chat. Uwe Johnson died at the age of forty-nine. I doubt whether this author and his work are currently taken as a yard-stick. In his work we could find out what literature, besides the celebration of subjective states of mind, can reflect and refract, facetted and reassembled from fragments; find out how the barbarity of our time has been made palatable, how each crime justifies the next; contemporary history and its flotsam and jetsam on every shore. Uwe Johnson proves how devoted service to the demands of the epic can be transformed into great literature. Instead of recognising this we deal today in literary small change; or even more shabbily, this much-polished small coin is placed in circulation as the currency of post-modernism in after-dinner speeches, yet it is little more than the Ego's sneezing hay fever.

Whether to provide a personal refutation of my all-too-German conclusions or to put my most recent reading experiences to the test of my current subject, I wish to single out a writer who has a different temperament from Uwe Johnson, God knows, and who has shaped the history of his native lands into two epic assaults – Salman Rushdie and his novels, *Midnight's Children* and *Shame*.

At midnight on 15 August 1947, as India became independent, midnight's children came into the world. Rushdie has endowed them with wonderful gifts so that in a fantastical way they grow up as contemporaries of the emerging Indian state. It is a period marked by hatred, pogroms, wars, famines, partitions, which the author offers in story and counter-story, drowns in floods of words, steeps in corrosive satire, and elevates to myths which end in sewers.

On the journey to Bombay, the scene of all Rushdie's fiction, Saleem (midnight's hero) reports events that happened shortly before his birth:

> On June 4th, my ill-matched parents left for Bombay by Frontier Mail. (There were bangings, voices hanging on for dear life, fists crying out, 'Muharaj! Open, for one tick only! Ohé, from the milk of your kindness, great sir, do us favour!' And there was also – hidden beneath dowry in a green tin trunk – a forbidden, lapis-lazuli-encrusted, delicately-wrought silver spittoon.) On the same day, Earl Mountbatten of Burma held a press conference at which he announced the Partition of India, and hung his countdown calendar on the wall: seventy days to go to the transfer of power . . . sixty-nine . . . sixty-eight . . . tick, tock.

This manner of chewing over political events, and especially the pompous great moments of politics, and absorbing them into the digestive tract of literature, had to arouse revulsion: it made enemies for Salman Rushdie in India and Pakistan. His polemic against Indira Ghandi and her sterilisation programme starts off satirically, becomes suddenly direct in an aggressive manner, and finally whips itself up to a hellish spectre which releases laughter as if the Prime Minister were possessed by the black goddess Kali.

Rushdie opens his invective against 'the Widow' with witty banter:

> Influence of hair styles on the course of history: there's another ticklish business. If William Methwold had lacked a centre-parting, I might not have been here today; and if the Mother of the

Nation had had a coiffure of uniform pigment, the Emergency she spawned might easily have lacked a darker side. But she had white hair on one side and black on the other; the Emergency, too, had a white part – public, visible, documented, a matter for historians – and a black part which, being secret macabre untold, must be a matter for us.

This indicates in classic manner the position of the writer whenever he uses history as his material. He wants to bring the obverse and obscure side to light. He burrows in refugees' luggage, he pokes around in the faeces of the powerful. No corpse is too sacred for him; he has to plunder it. His view of contemporary events is wilfully rash and seeks to capture politics before it disguises itself as history. He is forever cleaning down facades, digging up foundations. And when he sends society's loveliest conventions flying, it is crows and even vultures who do the screeching.

You must also read at long last the great novel *Petals of Blood* by the African novelist, Ngugi Wa Thiong'o, who did his country (Kenya) the service of exposing the network of power and corruption of the colonial and post-colonial era. I quote at random from the book:

> The man who came to the office was the one who betrayed me and Nding'uri. He had, as I later gathered, a contract with the company to transport the company's goods all over. The clerks were saying after he had gone inside: Uhuru has really come. Before independence no African was allowed to touch the company's goods except as a labourer. Now Mr Kimeria handles millions!

Is Kenya too far away? Is not this network ours also? Is not our Herr Flick a king-sized version of the medium-sized Mr Kimeria? Would not the phalanx of the many Flicks who financed Hitler and extracted commercial advantage even from the inmates of concentration camps, together with the excessive number of Flicks who are now corrupting the Federal Republic of Germany, be worth a novel? A novel that would uncover from beneath pedestrianised zones the bog-hole which survived the Year Dot, the New Beginning, and from which every last one of us has emerged complacent if irritated by the lingering stench which cannot be dispelled, not even by brave and breezy gestures with the Constitution for a fan.

However, assuming that someone gifted with language were to write this novel, that a younger writer were to jump well-armed into the Flickmire and provoke it to blabber openly and blow up into bubbles of epic dimension . . . suppose the sick-named-Flick got between the covers of a book . . . what should my conjured author expect?

Let us disregard my own experiences: he could end up like Wolfgang Koeppen who published his novel *Das Treibhaus* [The Hothouse] at the end of the fifties and with it revealed the inner life of Bonn, the federal capital. Colportage, crude simplification, journalistic black-and-white portraiture, would be the accusations from the right; and the contemporary left (insofar as there is one) would either make post-modernist noises (following the spirit of the age) or comment on the absence of traditional class-oriented perspective. The assessment of committed contemporary literature would be as usual unanimous: the in – many – ways gifted writer lacks objectivity, but there isn't enough use of 'the whispering imperfect', bog-holes can be better written about after drainage. Furthermore the present day is showing itself to be far too trivial. Political jargon is getting out of control. Who in a hundred years' time wants to know who presided over what investigation committee, apart from which Flick and Kohl are self-caricatures and therefore not suitable material for literature?

Do I exaggerate? A quotation may prove that even our classics, as soon as they describe the present in all too exact detail, run the risk of being torn to pieces:

> At about four o'clock they returned from the excursion and stopped at the Prinz Regenten, an old tree-lined square which had always been called Triangle Square because of its shape. The election results were still far from certain; but it had already become clear that many progressive votes would go to the social democrat candidate Freilenhauser Torgelow who, though not present in person, nevertheless had the support of ordinary voters. Hundreds of his party's members were standing about in groups on Triangle Square and were talking and laughing about the election meetings that had been held during the previous few days,

some in the country and some in Rheinsberg and Wutz, by members of the opposition parties. One of those standing under the trees, an intimate of Torgelow's, was the wood-turner's journeyman, Derkopp, who recently had enjoyed a great reputation simply in his capacity as a wood-turner's journeyman. Everyone thought 'He could even be a Bebel. Why not? Bebel is old and then we would have him.' But Derkopp really knew how to stir people.

You will have recognised this already; this and much more is what Theodor Fontane wrote in his last novel *Der Stechlin* [named after a character] which was published in the year of his death (1898), and greeted by furious reviewers. Things like elections don't belong to literature especially when the elections are won by socialists, not suitable material for literature.

Nowadays we read Fontane's novels retrospectively, as if in all their discursive variety they were written at a remove from any present day. We have forgotten equally quickly just how much venom was poured out by German critics, when Thomas Mann did not return from exile, but came back with *Doctor Faustus* to haul the Germans over the coals.

Books of this type – I have cited examples – are painful. They repel and provoke because they tax the reader consistently with another present day, the 'once upon a time' notwithstanding. Our subject, 'history reflected in the literature of its day', cannot encompass the entire range of literary production. In offering examples only from prose works for the sake of brevity, I am aware that numerous poems, plays, diaries and autobiographies have had to be omitted. I am thinking of Hochhuth's *The Representative*, of the post-war diary of Max Frisch, but also of Gottfried Benn's still horrifying lecture of 1933, 'Der neue Staat und die Intellektuellen'. The force of their contemporary witness could be discussed in the course of this congress and so, I hope, our foreign visitors may be spared in-fighting between the two German states as our dominant theme.

The torments of our era are more comprehensive that our own proscribed national preoccupations. Under the protection of the two great powers, which has now become an affliction, weighed down by the growing armaments' burden and the corresponding increase in misery, the human race lives from day to day in the face of impending self-destruction. Literature cannot withdraw from this existential position unless it is prepared to succumb to the *Zeitgeist* and lose itself in the non-committal attitudes on which video culture thrives. Then it would be literature no longer but at best a sensitive appendage to the entertainment industry.

Just six months ago in New York the international PEN conference illustrated how powerless we writers are against being forced into the political strait-jackets of communism and anti-communism. At the conference were Amos Oz from Israel; the simultaneously Indian, Pakistani, and British Salman Rushdie; and not least among the others Breyten Breytenbach and Nadine Gordimer from South Africa, who commanded an audience for the distress and need in their countries.

When Breytenbah briefly left his Parisian exile to return to his native land (for which, between 1975 and 1982, he had been only good enough for prison) to collect a literary prize he, the man who has captured the history of South Africa in a thousand mirror fragments, gave an address of which we have also taken careful note. My final quotation is from this manifesto:

> The white political caste will some day stand in the dock of history and be condemned for crimes perpetrated by a minority which in its confusion considered itself to be something special, for corruption of the values and standards of a civilised world, for the wanton destruction of a country.

EDWARD BOND

Song

The gallows stand high in South Africa
They're hanging five blacks tomorrow
The roar of trade in the market place
Will drown the wails of sorrow
The whiteman boss will turn in his bed
And snatch five minutes more
When the lever is pulled the trapdoor will fall
And five blackmen will be dead

The gallows stand high in South Africa
A few traders pack up their stalls
In the night the radar screens flicker
And sentries tramp on the walls
The whiteman boss turns over in bed
And dreams of his land divine
And murmurs as he stirs in his sleep
It's mine mine mine mine mine

The gallows stand high in South Africa
Share prices are keeping up well
The armoured cars stand guard in the streets
It's a peaceful morning in hell
The whiteman boss dreams of his land
Flowing with milk and honey
But the land he rules with jambok and rope
Is flowing with blood and money

The prices stand high on the stock exchange
Though a few traders start to go
But shares in rope pay good dividends
And the gallows puts on a show
The whiteman boss sleeps on and sighs
Soon the morning will break
And as five blacks are hanged he'll hurry to work
On the make make make make make

They've taken the bodies down from the ropes
And laid them to rest on the ground
And deep in the mines where their brothers work
There's a rumbling tramping sound
And in England they're counting gold in their sleep
They don't wake though the rumbling grows loud
And the white-topped waves on their island shores
Turn into a shroud

This Is Not Prophecy

In the past the tyrant's last words were emptier than his victim's howls
His soldiers' bones lay heaped with their rusting weapons
His prisoners' children ran on the grass that grows over the pedestals
of his monuments
He stored nothing against time
His prisons are ruins and his images broken

But now there are new weapons: lasers and atoms
The seed swells monstrously in the husk – does not turn into fruit –
swells and remains seed – breaking the skin of the fruit – devouring
the pith and the rind as if the skeleton ate the skin that covered it
The seeds in the wheatears are vermin – the rain is the spit of snakes

The danger was never prisons and barracks and the stone monuments
that watch the living
Children survive their parents' death by torture or famine
Our danger is not the sword but the word
Our danger is the doctrine
Beasts of the field and forest go on all fours or creep on their bellies
each after its nature
But we become what we learn
This is the tyrant's teaching:
        I am the Zion of culture and men are beasts of the city
        I am the stone image radiant as water

My stone face stands against change and my stone mouth speaks laws
The generations of people are sand-driven by wind – sifted to dust by fire – turned to the earth's mud by rain
Ignorance is taught in the tyrant's schools and broadcast on his screens
Great lies are published
The human image is corrupted so that the lines on our face become the spoor of beasts – the tracks of animals fighting in the city and flecking the dust with their blood
And from this teaching come all wars
War is always a prophecy that fulfils itself
Only false prophecies become true
They slide with the knife-edge of water under the dreamer's door
The prison wall has two sides: those on the outside are locked in the prison
Who will escape from the outside?
Only lies are mighty
It is our strength and weakness that we become what we are taught

What have you prisoners to do with me
I am not shut in your prison – I pass the torturer in the street – I eat
I will not die of your wounds – I do not groan under your sufferings
Why should I be concerned with your sufferings?
Suffer if your time calls you!

Yet my fear is greater than your fear and my danger as great
I cannot survive false doctrine
The sword-blade is short and bullets grope in the air like blindmen's fingers
But there is no limit to the corruption caused by false doctrine
Already the rulers retreat to their bunkers as if they ruled the world from the grave
They have new weapons – they will use them: it is the mark of the tyrant that he uses his weapons
The tyrant's tongue is a net – he will speak – he will cast
And his ten thousand ten thousand fists will haul the future into his maw
The lie is mighty: it will devour the unborn

The prophecy will kill generations
He imprisons the seed: it will give birth to bones and teeth
No one can survive false doctrine
The prophecy that comes true is false
I am afraid

Lies are mighty – truth is not mighty
It is small as the human hand and as fragile as children's games
But under the tyrant the slaves are free
Only they do not learn false doctrine
Only they do not see all men in the torturer's image
The wind whistles over the barbwire like the hangman calling to his
assistants
But the prison protects its prisoners: they are free
The torturer straps down his victims: they are free
The hungry child eats the emptiness of his bowl: he is fed
Such are our times
I stand among the last generations
I am afraid
This is not prophecy
Free us you prisoners!
Feed us you starving!
Teach us you slaves!

DANIIL KHARMS

The Drawback
(translated from Russian by Neil Cornwell)

Pronin said:
– You have very beautiful stockings.
Irina Mazer said:
– Do you like my stockings?
Pronin said:
– Oh yes. Very much. – And he made a grab at them with his hand.
Irina said:
– But why do you like my stockings?
Pronin said:
– They are very smooth.
Irina lifted her skirt and said:
– And do you see how high they go?
Pronin said:
– Oh yes, I do.
Irina said:
– But here they come to an end. Up here it's bare leg.
– Oh, and what leg! – said Pronin.
– I've got very thick legs, – said Irina. – And I'm very wide in the hips.
– Show me, – said Pronin.
– I can't, – said Irina, – I've no knickers on.
Pronin got down on his knees in front of her.
Irina said:
– What are you kneeling for?
Pronin kissed her on the leg, a little above the stocking top, and said:
– That's what for.
Irina said:
– Why are you lifting my skirt even higher? I've already told you
I've no knickers on.
But Pronin lifted her skirt all the same and said:
– Never mind, never mind.
– What do you mean, never mind? – said Irina.
But at this juncture someone was knocking at the door. Irina
briskly pulled down her skirt, and Pronin got up from the floor
and went over to the window.

– Who's there? – asked Irina, through the door.
– Open the door, – said a sharp voice.
Irina opened the door and into the room came a man in a black
coat and high boots. Behind him came a pair of soldiers of the
lowest rank, rifles at the ready, and behind them came the caretaker.
The lower ranks stood by the door, while the man in the black
coat went up to Irina Mazer and said:
– Your name?
– Mazer, – said Irina.
– Your name? – asked the man in the black coat, turning to Pronin.
Pronin said:
– My name is Pronin.
– Do you have a weapon? – asked the man in the black coat.
– No, – said Pronin.
– Sit down here, – said the man in the black coat, indicating a chair
to Pronin.
Pronin sat down.
– And you, – said the man in the black coat, turning to Irina,
– put your coat on. You'll have to come for a ride with us.
– What for? – asked Irina.
The man in the black coat did not reply.
– I'll need to change, – said Irina.
– No, – said the man in the black coat.
– But there's something else I need to put on, – said Irina.
– No, – said the man in the black coat.
Irina put on her fur coat in silence.
– Good-bye, then – she said to Pronin.
– Conversations are not allowed, – said the man in the black coat.
– Do I come with you as well? – asked Pronin.
– Yes, – said the man in the black coat. – Get your coat on.
Pronin stood up, took his coat and hat down from the peg, put
them on and said:
– Well, I'm ready.
– Let's go, – said the man in the black coat.
The lower ranks and the caretaker stamped their feet.
They all went out into the corridor.
The man in the black coat locked the door of Irina's room and
sealed it with two brown seals.

– Outside, – he said.
And they all went out of the flat, loudly slamming the outside door.

12 November 1940

A Commentary by Neil Cornwell

Daniil Kharms was the pen name of Daniil Ivanovich Yuvachov (1905-1942), the son of a minor St Petersburg religious and literary figure. He achieved a certain local renown as a Leningrad eccentric and a writer of children's stories in the 1920s and '30s. Kharms's activities with the avant-garde OBERIU (Association of Real Art), as performer and author of absurdist prose, verse and drama, are much less well known due to Stalinist policies of enforced disbandment and silence (and worse!) Even these 'adult' works of Kharms, striking in the bizarre use of violence, falling and other forms of the unexpected, usually retain a childlike simplicity and brevity.

The shadow of arrest hangs over many works by Kharms: the prose miniatures (or 'incidents' — *sluchai* — as he termed them) and the play *Yelizaveta Bam*. It hung too over Kharms himself. He was arrested and exiled, first in 1931, and again in wartime Leningrad in 1941 when (it is reported) the caretaker of his block called him down, in his bedroom slippers, 'for a few minutes'. He died in prison, probably of starvation, in February 1942. A subsequent shadow of arrest lingered over Kharms scholarship. The Leningrad scholar Mikhail Meylakh was arrested in 1983, for alleged activities ostensibly unconnected with his Kharms publications abroad. British-made handcuffs, it is reported by an impeccable source, are in common use in the Gulag.

Happily, Meylakh was released in a 1987 amnesty and the era of *glasnost* has now led to substantial publications of Kharms in the Soviet Union. Elsewhere, a Yugoslav director has made a surreal film of 'The Kharms Case'! Less happily, the worldwide demand for British-made handcuffs does not diminish.

MEDBH MC GUCKIAN

No Streets, No Numbers

The wind bruises the curtains' jay blue stripes
Like an unsold fruit or a child who writes
Its first word. The rain tonight in my hair
Runs a firm unmuscular hand over something
Sand-ribbed and troubled, a desolation
That could erase all memory of warmth
From the patch of vegetation where torchlight
Has fallen. The thought that I might miss
Even a second of real rain is like the simple
Double knock of the stains of birth and death,
Two men back to back carrying furniture
From a room on one side of the street
To a room on the other. And the weather
Is a girl with woman's eyes like a knife-wound
In her head – such is a woman's very deep
Violation as a woman, not like talk,
Not like footsteps, already a life crystallises
Round it, and time that is so often only a word,
'Later, later', spills year into year like three days'
Post, or the drawing-room with the wall
Pulled down.

I look into the endless settees
Of the talk-dried drawing-room where all
The colours are wrong. Is that because
I unshaded all the lamps so their sunny
Unhurt movements would be the colour
Of emotions which have no adventures?
But I'm afraid of the morning most,
Which stands like a chance of life
On a shelf, or a ruby velvet dress
Cut to the middle of the back
That can be held on the shoulder by a diamond lizard.

A stone is nearly a perfect secret, always
By itself though it touches so much, shielding
Its heart beyond its strong curtain of ribs
With its arm. Not that I want you
To tell me what you have not told anyone:
How your narrow house propped up window
After window while the light sank and sank.
Why your edges though they shine
No longer grip precisely like other people.
How sometimes the house won and sometimes
The sea-coloured sea-clear dress,
Made new from one over a hundred years old,
That foamed away the true break
In the year, leaving the house
Masterless and flagless. That dream
Of a too early body undamaged
And beautiful, head smashed to pulp,
Still grows in my breakfast cup;
It used up the sore red of the applebox,
It nibbled at the fortnight of our violent
Christmas like a centenarian fir-tree.
I talk as if the evenings had been fine,
The roof of my shelves not broken
Like an oath on crossed rods,
Or I had not glimpsed myself
As the Ides of September white
At the telephone. Two sounds
Spin together and fight for sleep
Between the bed and the floor,
An uneasy clicking to of unsorted
Lawn-blue plates, the friction
Of a skirt of hands refusing to let go.
And how am I to break into
This other life, this small eyebrow,
Six inches off mine, which has been
Blown from my life like the most aerial
Of birds? If the summer that never burnt
And began two days ago is ashes now,
Autumn's backbone will have the pallor

Of the snowdrop, the shape of the stone
Showing in the wall. Our first summer-time
Night we will sit out drinking
On the pavement of Bird Street
Where we kissed in the snow, as the day
After a dream in which one really was
In love teases out the voice reserved for children.

Something Called Sleep

Sleep pours from a jug held at a height
In the angle of a hand, as the moon inhales
The world into which the present will soon fall.

Darkness takes the colour of colours back
And back from a much-shaded house to dawn's
Great nakedness, breathing only once a minute.

Through the gossamer walls of a fourteen-year-old,
The long afternoons burn like a verandah
Running along two sides with no interiors.

A month of mountains honeycombs the broken
Spell of her breast, a week of windows lets them
More into her secret than they want to be.

I tap the tablemats sharply on edge,
A lady painted full length with the eyelashes,
Her instrument, the last important flower of the year.

SAMUEL BECKETT

Murderous Humanitarianism
(*from the original French of The Surrealist Group in Paris*)

For centuries the soldiers, priests and civil agents of imperialism, in a welter of looting, outrage and wholesale murder, have battened with impunity on the coloured races; now it is the turn of the demagogues, with their counterfeit liberalism.

But the proletariat of today, whether metropolitan or colonial, is no longer to be fooled by fine words as to the real end in view, which is still, as it always was, the exploitation of the greatest number for the benefit of a few slavers. Now these slavers, knowing their days to be numbered and reading the doom of their system in the world crisis, fall back on a gospel of mercy, whereas they rely more than ever on their traditional methods of slaughter to enforce their tyranny.

No great penetration is required to read between the lines of the news, whether in print or on the screen: punitive expeditions, blacks lynched in America, the white scourge devastating town and country in our parliamentary kingdoms and bourgeois republics.

War, that reliable colonial endemic, receives fresh impulse in the name of 'pacification'. France may well be proud of having launched this godsent euphemism at the precise moment when, in throes of pacifism, she sent forth her tried and trusty thugs with instructions to plunder all those distant and defenceless peoples from whom the intercapitalistic butchery had distracted her attentions for a space.

The most scandalous of these wars, that against the Riffains in 1925, stimulated a number of intellectuals, investors in militarism, to assert their complicity with the hangmen of jingo and capital.

Responding to the appeal of the Communist party we protested against the war in Morocco and made our declaration in *Revolution first and always*.

In a France hideously inflated from having dismembered Europe, made mincemeat of Africa, polluted Oceania and ravaged whole tracts of Asia, we Surréalistes pronounced ourselves in favour of changing the imperialist war, in its chronic and colonial form, into a civil war. Thus we placed our energies at the disposal of the revolution, of the proletariat and its struggles, and defined our attitude towards the colonial problem, and hence towards the colour question.

Gone were the days when the delegates of this snivelling capitalism might screen themselves in those abstractions which, in both secular and religious mode, were invariably inspired by the christian ignominy and which strove on the most grossly interested grounds to masochise whatever peoples had not yet been contaminated by the sordid moral and religious codes in which men feign to find authority for the exploitation of their fellows.

When whole peoples had been decimated with fire and the sword it became necessary to round up the survivors and domesticate them in such a cult of labour as could only proceed from the notions of original sin and atonement. The clergy and professional philanthropists have always collaborated with the army in this bloody exploitation. The colonial machinery that extracts the last penny from natural advantages hammers away with the joyful regularity of a poleaxe. The white man preaches, doses, vaccinates, assassinates and (from himself) receives absolution. With his psalms, his speeches, his guarantees of liberty, equality and fraternity, he seeks to drown the noise of his machine-guns.

It is no good objecting that these periods of rapine are only a necessary phase and pave the way, in the words of the time-honoured formula, 'for an era of prosperity founded on a close and intelligent collaboration between the natives and the metropolis!' It is no good trying to palliate collective outrage and butchery by jury in the new colonies by inviting us to consider the old, and the peace and prosperity they have so long enjoyed. It is no good blustering about the Antilles and the 'happy evolution' that has enabled them to be assimilated, or very nearly, by France.

In the Antilles, as in America, the fun began with the total extermination of the natives, in spite of their having extended a most cordial reception to the Christopher Colombian invaders. Were they now, in the hour of triumph, and having come so far, to set out empty handed for home? Never! So they sailed on to Africa and stole men. These were in due course promoted by our humanists to the ranks of slavery, but were more or less exempted from the sadism of their masters in virtue of the fact that they represented a capital which had to be safeguarded like any other capital. Their descendants, long since reduced to destitution (in the French Antilles they live on vegetables and salt cod and are dependent in the matter of clothing on whatever old guano sacks they are lucky enough to steal), constitute a black proletariat whose conditions of life are even more wretched than those of its European equivalent and which is exploited by a coloured bourgeoisie quite as ferocious an any other. This bourgeoisie, covered by the machine-guns of culture, 'elects' such perfectly adequate representatives as 'Hard Labour' Diagne and 'Twister' Delmont.

The intellectuals of this new bourgeoisie, though they may not all be specialists in parliamentary abuse, are no better than the experts when they proclaim their devotion to the Spirit. The value of this idealism is precisely given by the manoeuvres of its doctrinaires who, in their paradise of comfortable iniquity, have organised a system of poltroonery proof against all the necessities of life and the urgent consequences of dream. These gentlemen, votaries of corpses and theosophies, go to ground in the past, vanish down the warrens of Himalayan monasteries. Even for those whom a few last shreds of shame and intelligence dissuade from invoking those current religions whose God is too frankly a God of cash, there is the call of some 'mystic Orient' or other. Our gallant sailors, policemen and agents of imperialistic thought, in labour with opium and literature, have swamped us with their irretentions of nostalgia; the function of all these idyllic alarums among the dead and gone being to distract our thoughts from the present, the abominations of the present.

A Holy-Saint-faced *International* of hypocrites deprecates the material progress foisted on the blacks, protests, courteously, against the importation not only of alcohol, syphillis and field artillery, but also of railways and printing. This comes well after the former rejoicings of its evangelical spirit at the idea that the 'spirtual values' current in capitalistic societies, and notably the respect of human life and property, would devolve naturally from enforced familiarity with fermented drinks, firearms and disease. It is scarcely necessary to add that the colonist demands this respect of property without reciprocity.

Those blacks who have merely been compelled to distort in terms of fashionable jazz the natural expression of their joy at finding themselves partakers of a universe from which western peoples have wilfully withdrawn may consider themselves lucky to have suffered no worse thing than degradation. The eighteenth century derived nothing from China except a repertory of frivolities to grace the alcove. In the same way the whole object of our romantic exoticism and modern travel-lust is of use only in entertaining that class of blasé client sly enough to see an interest in deflecting to his own advantage the torrent of those energies which soon, much sooner than he thinks, will close over his head.

André Breton, Roger Caillois, René Char,
René Crevel, Paul Eluard, J.-M. Monnerot,
Benjamin Péret, Yves Tanguy, André Thirion,
Pierre Unik, Pierre Yoyotte.

JOHN BANVILLE

Testimony
(*from* The Book of Evidence, *a novel in progress*)

My lord, when you ask me to tell the court in my own words, this is what I shall say. I am kept locked up here like some exotic animal, last survivor of a species they had thought extinct. They should let in people to view me, the girleater, svelte and dangerous, padding to and fro in my cage, my terrible green glance flickering past the bars, give them something to dream about, tucked up cosy in their beds of a night. After my capture they clawed at each other to get a look at me. They would have paid for the privilege, I believe. They shouted abuse, and shook their fists at me, showing their teeth. It was unreal, somehow, frightening yet comic, the sight of them there, milling on the pavement like extras, young men in cheap raincoats, and women with shopping bags, and one or two silent, grizzled characters who just stood, fixed on me hungrily, haggard with envy. Then a guard threw a blanket over my head and bundled me into a squad car. I laughed. There was something irresistibly funny in the way reality, banal, literal-minded as ever, was fulfilling my worst fantasies.

By the way, that blanket. Did they bring it specially, or do they always keep one handy in the boot? Such questions trouble me now, I brood on them. What an interesting figure I must have cut, glimpsed there, sitting up in the back like a sort of mummy, as the car sped through the sunlit, evening streets, bleating importantly.

Then this place. It was the noise that first of all impressed me. A terrible racket, yells and whistles, hoots of laughter, arguments, sobs. But there are moments of stillness, too, as if a great fear, or a great sadness, has fallen suddenly, striking us all speechless. The air stands motionless in the corridors, like stagnant water. It is laced with a faint, fine stink of carbolic, which bespeaks the charnel house. In the beginning I fancied it was me, I mean I thought this smell was mine, my contribution. Perhaps it is? The daylight too is strange, even outside, in the yard, as if something has happened to it, as if something has been done to it, before it is allowed to reach us. It has an acid, lemony cast, and comes in two intensities, either it is not enough to see by or it sears the sight. Of the various kinds of darkness

I shall not speak.

Remand prisoners are assigned the best cells. This is as it should be. After all, I might be found innocent. Oh, I mustn't laugh, it hurts my ribs where Sergeant what's-his-name punched me – a matter on which, incidentally, I shall have something to say when I get into the witness box. I have a table and what they call an easy chair. There is even a television set, though I rarely watch it, now that my case is *sub judice* and there is nothing about me on the news. The sanitation facilities, it is true, leave something to be desired. Slopping out: how apt, these phrases. I must see if I can get a catamite, or do I mean a neophyte? Some young fellow, nimble and willing, and not too fastidious. That shouldn't be difficult. I must see if I can get a dictionary, too.

I confess I had hopelessly romantic expectations of how things would be in here. Somehow I pictured myself a sort of celebrity, kept apart from the other prisoners in a special wing, where I would receive parties of grave, important people and hold forth to them about the great issues of the day, impressing the men and charming the ladies. What insight! What breadth! They said you were a beast, cold blooded, cruel, but now that we have seen you, have heard you, why –! And I, striking an elegant pose, my ascetic profile lifted to the light in the barred window, fingering a scented handkerchief and faintly smirking, Jean-Jacques the cultured killer.

Not like that, not like that at all. But not like other clichés either. Where are the mess-hall riots, the mass break-outs, that kind of thing, so familiar from the silver screen? What of the scene in the exercise yard in which the stoolie is done to death with a shiv while a pair of blue-jawed heavyweights stage a diversionary fight? When are the gang-bangs going to start? The fact is, in here is like out there, only more so. We are obsessed with physical comfort. The place is always overheated, we might be in an incubator, yet there are endless complaints of draughts and sudden chills and frozen feet at night. Food is important too, we pick over our plates of mush, sniffing and sighing, as if we were a convention of gourmets. After a parcel delivery word goes round like wildfire. Psst! She sent him a battenberg! Homemade! It's all just like school, really, the mixture of misery and cosiness, the numbed longing, the noise, and everywhere, always, that particular smelly grey warm male fug.

It was different, I'm told, when the politicals were here. They used to frog-march up and down the corridors, barking at each other in bad Irish, causing much merriment among the ordinary criminals. But then they all went on hunger strike or something, and were moved away to a place of their own, and life returned to normal.

Why are we so compliant? Is it the stuff they are said to put in our tea to dull the libido? Or is it the drugs? Your honour, I know that no one, not even the jury, likes a squealer, but I think it is my duty to inform the court of the brisk trade in proscribed substances which is carried on in this institution. There are screws, I mean warders, involved in it, I can supply their numbers if requested. Anything can be had, uppers and downers, tranqs, horse, crack, you name it – not that you, of course, your worship, are likely to be familiar with these terms from the lower depths, I have only learned them myself since coming here. As you would imagine, it is mainly the younger men who indulge. One recognises them, stumbling along the gangways like somnambulists, with that little, wistful, stunned smile of the truly zonked. There are some, however, who do not smile, who seem indeed as if they will never smile again. They are the lost ones, the goners. They stand gazing off, with a blank, preoccupied expression, the way that injured animals look away from us, mutely, as if we are mere phantoms to them, whose pain is taking place in a different world from ours.

But no, it's not just the drugs. Something essential has gone, the stuffing has been knocked out of us. We are not exactly men any more. Old lags, fellows who have committed some really impressive crimes, sashay about the place like dowagers, pale, soft, pigeon-chested, big in the beam. They squabble over library books, some of them even knit. The young too have their hobbies, they sidle up to me in the recreation room, their calf eyes fairly brimming, and shyly display their handiwork. If I have to admire one more ship in a bottle I shall scream. Still, they are so sad, so vulnerable, these muggers, these rapists, these baby-batterers. When I think of them I always picture, I'm not sure why, that strip of stubbly grass and one tree that I can glimpse from my window if I press my cheek against the bars and peer down diagonally past the wire and the wall.

PATRICK GALVIN

Letter to a Political Prisoner

Behind the fences of barbed wire
Behind iron bars
Locked in your cell
Under stone walls –
Wherever you are, my friend,
I can see your face.

I send you a towel
Wrapped in olive leaves.
Press it to your eyes
And let the image remain
Embedded forever
In a crucifixion of cloth.

Sometimes, my friend,
When the rain falls in my country
And the upturned faces of my people
Weep towards the sun
I tell them I have seen the sun
In darker places and in catacombs of ice.

I send you my love.
I send you a flag weaved
Without pain or nationality.
I send you my heart
Cradled forever
In a handful of rain.

Sleep well, my friend,
And when they wake you in the morning
Tell them you have slept bone to bone
And mouth to mouth
And stone to stone.
Tell them that you are not alone.

I send you a lamp
I send you my hand raised
Against the bleeding of our kind.
I send you a storm –
Raging forever
Against the iniquities of the blind.

GOFRAIDH FIONN Ó DÁLAIGH (d. 1387)

A Child in Prison
(*translated from Irish by Thomas Kinsella*)

A pregnant woman (sorrow's sign)
once there was, in painful prison.
The God of Elements let her bear
in prison there a little child.

The little boy, when he was born,
grew up like any other child
(plain as we could see him there)
for a space of years, in prison.

That the woman was a prisoner
did not lower the baby's spirits.
She minded him, though in prison,
like one without punishment or pain.

Nothing of the light of day
(O misery!) could they see
but the bright ridge of a field
through a hole someone had made.

Yet the loss was not the same
for the son as for the mother:
her fair face failed in form
while the baby gained in health.

The child, raised where he was,
grew better by his bondage,
not knowing in his fresh frail limbs
but prison was ground of Paradise.

He made little playful runs
while her spirits only deepened.
(Mark well, lest you regret,
these deeds of son and mother.)

He said one day, beholding
a tear on her lovely face:
'I see the signs of sadness;
now let me hear the cause.'

'No wonder that I mourn,
my foolish child,' said she.
'This cramped place is not our lot,
and suffering pain in prison.'

'Is there another place,' he said,
'lovelier than ours?
Is there a brighter light than this
that your grief grows so heavy?'

'For I believe,' the young child said,
'mother, although you mourn,
we have our share of light.
Don't waste your thoughts in sorrow.'

'I do not wonder at what you say,
young son,' the girl replied.
'You think this is a hopeful place
because you have seen no other.

'If you knew what I have seen
before this dismal place
you would be downcast also
in your nursery here, my soul.'

'Since it is you know best, lady,'
the little child replied,
'hide from me no longer
what more it was you had.'

'A great outer world in glory
formerly was mine.
After that, beloved boy,
my fate is a darkened house.'

At home in all his hardships,
not knowing a happier state,
fresh-cheeked and bright, he did not grudge
the cold and desolate prison.

And so is the moral given:
the couple there in prison
are the people of the world,
imprisoned life their span.

Compared with joy in the Son of God
in His everlasting realm
an earthly mansion is only grief,
prisoners all the living.

THOMAS KINSELLA

A Portrait of the Artist

We might have guessed it would end in argument
and the personal. Those acid exchanges
hoarse in the hall: An architect
is an artist! His first duty is beauty!
Finding our way down the steps in the small hours
and walking up the terrace in relief.

A movement of memory across the road.
A pair of shades the other side of the Canal:
They had reached the canal bank
and, turning from their course, came on by the trees.
About there. Two youthful dead. Walking
in ghost dispute along the farther bank.

The one, with the lighter touch, possessed, nagging
beauty into its place among the senses.
And the Fool lending a quick ear, tittering
but honoured: *What is beauty?*

*

The fugitive in its accident, exact;
a structure fixed and lasting.
                          A jewel of process
turned around on the fingers to be admired.
Often recogniseable by a start
of certainty beyond the understanding.

My fingers, at the front gate, stopped an instant
against your living skin in the night air.
A car prowled over the Bridge in a slow curve
under the lamp, then back across the Canal;
another came exactly on its track
with the same turn, the tail lights pulsing rose.

A soul roused herself out of the shades
in red and black leatherette. Another pair
waited in short skirts against the railings
under the graveyard trees, their cigarettes
pointing in the night. Their hidden eyes
wet to my senses; and their oyster mouths.

Three Irish Travellers in Black America

HUBERT BUTLER
In the Deep South (1962)

The best way to visit the Southern states is by Greyhound Bus on a tourist ticket (this trip was given to me by Riordan's Travel Agency in Limerick and I am everlastingly grateful to them). The Southern bus terminals have in recent years become historic battlefields, at which victories for the negro peoples as momentous as Marathon have been peaceably won. If you bus across Alabama from Atlanta to Jackson, Mississippi, you are following the route of one of the Rev. Martin Luther King's campaigns. He and his band of black and white Freedom Riders had embarked on a crusade to open for their people the Greyhound Bus white waiting-rooms, toilets, cafeterias, which had hitherto been regarded as race sanctuaries. At every stop they had met embattled waitresses, policemen, bus officials, and peacefully defied them. As they approached Jackson, resistance had been toughened by telephone, there were more and more police and finally the sanctuaries were locked, to the great discomfort of segregationist and integrationist alike. When the crusaders reached Jackson, they were all put in gaol. But the battle had been won. You very rarely see WHITES ONLY notices now, though I was surprised to find in the fine museum of Jackson a drinking tap labelled WHITE. Yet there is progress even there, for till recently the negroes were not allowed into the museum at all. The negro leaders have become expert and assured strategists, their telephones are always ringing, they look exhausted but happy. They hatch plots from which very tiny chickens emerge, but vast possibilities of growth are envisaged.

When in Atlanta, I met Wyatt Tee Walker, Luther King's second-in-command; he had just returned, famished and sleepless but exhilirated, from Albany in Southern Georgia; he had dashed down there to give moral support to some hundreds of negroes, who had been kneeling, praying, demonstrating outside the court house in which some Freedom Riders had been condemned. 'A sandwich please from the café next door!' he said to his office boy, as he collapsed into his chair, 'and one for this gentleman too! I am sorry,' he added to me, 'that I can't take you to lunch there, but it is segregated. However, we're tackling that next. I am giving them an ultimatum. If they don't desegregate within thirty days I'll organise a sit-in there.'

The next negro leader whom I met was keen-featured and vivacious like Mr Walker, and not very dark, so I decided to ask him an embarrassing question. He was the editor of a negro paper in Jackson, claiming to be 'the only negro paper in the States, which is not an Uncle Tom paper.' In parenthesis, Mrs Beecher Stowe, like most conciliatory people, annoyed both sides. She wanted the negros to be free, but expected them to be simple and merry like Uncle Tom and very deferential to the 'good' whites. So to be called 'an Uncle Tom paper' is to be damned.

My question was : 'I was told by an official of the White Citizens' Council' that you negro leaders are all partly white and therefore quite untypical. Is this so?' He answered quickly: 'More than 65 per cent of American negroes have white blood. I myself am part Indian and had a white grandfather.' In fact the average negro integrationist is not interested in racism and Africa. He smiles sardonically, when he hears the whites talk of a basic physical repugnance between black and white, for he knows that the white man invariably took the initiative in the creation of the 65 per cent. There was indeed a celebrated annual ball at New Orleans, still mentioned in the guidebook, attended by white men and black girls only. No marriages resulted from such sociabilities but many babies, who were brought up as slaves. In the Natchez area of Mississippi many of the more educated blacks and whites have mixed blood, because of an honourable and wealthy planter, who, unlike others, cared deeply for his parti-coloured off-spring and left them large marriage portions, which other planter families were very ready to share.

But the tradition of a deep racial antipathy persists in the South. It is blasphemous and even dangerous to question it. A clergyman in South Carolina told me that his congregation would mostly refuse to take communion with negroes, believing that it was a violation of a natural law to eat with them. Many Southern Baptists think that the posterity of Ham were cursed by Noah and even cultured white Southerners have scruples, unknown in the North, about sharing hairdressers with negroes. 'They want kinks taken out of their hair, WE want kinks put in,' is a common way of laughing off this intolerance. In a crowded New Orleans bus a friend and I were sharing a seat for three with a negro, when two tired-looking elderly ladies, hung with parcels, came in. We offered them our seats but they stared ahead with silent, stony dignity, as if we had not spoken. My friend explained that they were full of Southern pride and loyalty. 'How glad I am,' they were thinking, 'that dear Mother died before this day! What would Grandpa, who fell so gloriously at Vicksburg, have thought! Rather than lower the flag I will stand till I drop.'

As well as sit-ins, there are, of course, kneel-ins; when I was in Charleston most of the churches had been visited by bands of negroes. If they were admitted, they sat quietly in their pews and probably did not return. If they were turned away, there was a photographer present who immediately took photographs of the pious scuffle in the church porch and sent them to an integrationist newspaper. 'They're just exploiting religion for political purposes,' say the indignant segregationists. Who is right?

Two Churches stand out above all others in their consistently warm acceptance of the negro, the Roman Catholic and the Unitarian. Captious people say that it is easy for them to be tolerant, since they have so few negro adherents. I did not find this fair. The ministers of both faiths were ready to suffer criticism and obloquy for their belief that God created all men equal.

Probably there will now be no dramatic explosion of animosity or reconciliation. Most school integration is not very thorough in the South. If more than a few black children appear in a class, the whites move by degrees to some suburb, where there are no negroes with whom to integrate. Nor are the negroes all passionately integrationist, or very well-organised. Both sides are unhappy and confused. I saw a ladies' hat shop in New Orleans picketed by two earnest black students and one white. They carried banners, proclaiming a boycott of the shop because of its discrimination against negro employees, but behind the banners a group of black ladies, clucking happily over a selection of hats, was clearly visible.

If serious trouble were to arise, it would come not from the pacifist followers of Martin Luther King but from the Black Muslims. They number more than 100,000 'Black Men' in the USA. (They proudly proclaim themselves black and are not worried by the kinks in their hair.) They believe that Allah sent their late leader Elijah Muhammed to help them throw off the dominion of the whites. They are uncompromising and aggressive and have large resources. They thrive on racial tension and will doubtless disappear with it.

The negroes, by their numbers, are entitled, if democracy were enforced, to assume control of many of the Southern states. Their potential power is great. Their total annual income has been estimated at $20 billion, greater than the total income of Canada and greater than that of several European states. Yet people who have been humiliated and denied education do not make good rulers and their best friends do not anticipate a black Utopia. It is natural for the white Southerner to feel apprehension as the threat to his supremacy develops. He is exasperated by the tolerant detachment of the Yankees who see only the moral aspect of this complex historical tragedy.

BENEDICT KIELY
In the Week of Martin's Murder (1968/1977)

In Rathgar in the morning early, my son, John, wakes me up with some difficulty, and says 'But you wouldn't want to go back to Atlanta today. Somebody in Memphis has just murdered Martin Luther King.' Heavy head on the pillow I look at the ceiling and see dogwood blossom and see the days just gone, in number somewhere between seven and fourteen.

They began – a separate part of my life, never, I hope, nor the like of them, to be repeated – somewhere in the air over the furnaces of Birmingham, Alabama: and with the realisation that I really was on the way from Atlanta, Georgia, to Pomona, California, which is a sort of southerly part of Los Angeles. On the way to, of all things, an Irish week or a week of discussion on Irish literature. Organised by Darcy O'Brien (an American professor, critic, and novelist), and by the late W. R. Rodgers (Bertie, the poet); the guests being Dr Conor Cruise O'Brien, his wife, Dr Herbert Howarth (American professor and critic), and in a lesser capacity, obviously, myself.

Anyway: the plane is over Birmingham, Alabama, the man tells us. To my left, i.e. between me and the wall – sits an eighteen-year-old girl from Nowhere, Alabama, or the boondocks as they say. She is a young bride. When she was all of eight days married her husband, a soldier, was flown off to Vietnam. He now has his first furlough and is spending it in Honolulu. She is flying over to spend it with him, fare paid. The army, God help us all, looks after its own, as we also say of the devil. A second honeymoon she says. She is a sweet simple sort of a girl. On we go. It is her first time in an aeroplane.

Over the Mojave desert the plane turns on its side, not quite the whole way but almost. A woman screams, as in *Dangerous Dan McGrew*. A plastic cup out of which another woman is drinking takes off and hits against the slanting wall. Through a porthole or window, or whatever you call them in aeroplanes, I can see the Mojave desert, 35,000 feet down (we had earlier heard) and looking very harsh and like no place to land ass first. My own impulse is to scream or worse, but how can I when I'm practically lying on top of an eighteen-year-old Alabama girl whom I've just met for the first time and who has never been in a plane before? So I whisper into her right ear that this is what they call turbulence. She believes me and thus gives me great confidence in my narrative skill, or ability to tell lies in a moment of crisis.

The plane steadies itself. The captain says we are touching down in Las Vegas to take on more fuel. We touch down in Las Vegas. The desert winds blow. The mountains crouch back there like animals and look at us. The captain and his company take on no fuel. Men do something to one of the engines. For myself, a refuelling with four glasses of Jack Daniels helps me to reckon that, on the law of probability, if it didn't happen that time it won't happen next time: and we go on our way rejoicing – well not quite and I am seldom so glad to see any man I know as I am to see Darcy O'Brien waiting for me in Los Angeles, who brings me to Pomona where it is good to see, partways up a mountain and in a house among orange groves, Bertie Rodgers, the poet, as content as he ever was in an apple orchard in Armagh, when, that is, it was possible to be content there under the apples.

Then after an Irish week under the oranges, the long haul back again to Alabama. In Dallas where we touch down I stand up to stretch myself and walk towards the door and a fine tall young woman says I'm not allowed to disembark, or whatever they call it. So I tell her in jest, that I was never in Texas and that, back home in Ireland, I'd like to be able to lie to them and say I was. When to my amazement she says, 'Bully for you. I'm a Texan.' And she leads me out of the plane and off the tarmac until I can stand on earth, real earth, Texas to wit. The earth feels very good.

Touchdown again in Birmingham, Alabama, and a take-off with

what seems to be those blast furnaces red in the night below us and then Atlanta airport at two in the morning and my discovery that I haven't the price of my taxi home, and it's a long, long way. A black man takes pity on me and drives me and accepts my cheque. On the way we pass by the church of the father of Martin Luther King: in which church I had heard Pete Seeger sing about Lyndon Johnson wading deeper and deeper into the Big Muddy – allegorically Vietnam. And heard singers and fiddlers from the Cumberland mountains, and watched mountainy men dance putting their feet down very flat and heavy.

My driver is a part-time preacher or a part-time taximan and later in the day he has to meet me so that we can cash the cheque in my liquor store where I am well-known: he knows few places where a black man, not too well off, can cash a stranger's cheque. But he *did* trust *me*. So to rest for twenty-four plus hours until the longer half of my journey begins. For this is to New York, and then to Ireland to the wedding of my daughter, Mary, and then back to New York and back to Atlanta and back to my business, whatever it is, as a visiting writer in Emory University: and I lie on my bed in Rathgar and look at the ceiling and the Mojave desert and wonder if when I get back to Atlanta the place will be white as a unicorn with dogwood in blossom.

Like all great beauty, and as Valentin Iremonger when he was a young fellow said about the Spring, the dogwood stops you suddenly: one week the world is ordinary, next week the eyes dazzle. When I left it, Atlanta had been ordinary. But even more than Herrick's or anybody's daffodils the dogwood hastes away too soon and this year, I thought, hatred might have hastened the death of the unicorn: and would the murdered man's coffin, carried on an ordinary, rough, four-wheeled farm wagon, go through white dazzlement or an ordinary world. Or could any world in which such things happened be happily ordinary? All this was, remember, a little before we began to distinguish ourselves among the nations of the earth (taking our place among the nations of the earth) for happenings extraordinary.

So back wearily all the way to the El Quixote on 23rd Street where I am wiser than Icarus and realise that, for the moment, I have had my bellyful of flying. Martin Luther King lies dead in Memphis and the chase is on and a suspect car has been found abandoned in Atlanta: to which fine city I take off by train and the hell wtih aeroplanes. But it makes no difference. Every time the train rattles I see the Mojave desert. To this blessed day, at awkward moments or on bad mornings when the 46A bus, notorious for turbulence, takes a sharp turn here in Dublin, I see the desert down there, 35,000 feet down, through clear air.

But going south, the Georgian mountains and the deep dark forests afflict me not with the claustrophobia that you might expect but with vertigo. Here is Gainsville, Georgia, and I know I'm almost home, Gainsville, the Chicken Capital of the World, which turns to the railroad one of the world's most unseemly backsides and which is the home town of Lester Maddox who once kept a controversial (racially) restaurant and from whom I once had a most gracious letter. In Atlanta I know the elderly couple who taught Lester when he went to school: Horatio and Pansy Shappey, nice, simple people. A sober college-colleague of Scottish origin says, 'Taught him what?' And Lester now is singing, and telling corny jokes and playing the harmonica in a supper club in Sanford, Florida, in partnership with a black ex-convict called Bobby Lee Fears. This does not surprise me: it should be remembered of Lester that when in office he went out of his way to help the prisoners: and Bobby Lee Fears did wash dishes in that famous restaurant.

The journey is over and the dogwood is everywhere and the manhunt is on, and right around the very apartment I lived in. The fat young woman – she also comes from Alabama – in the apartment across the landing says that the rumour is that the wanted man spent a night in a hotel at the corner of Highland Avenue and the highway called after the Conquistador Ponce de Leon, who went in search of the seven golden cities. That's about a hundred yards away: the hotel, not the golden cities. They were never found. Spent a night in that hotel myself when I had just arrived and was waiting to find an apartment.

That rumour may or may not be true. But it is for sure true that men, presumably FBI men, have tapped on the door of every house and apartment in the area, shown an identikit picture and asked questions. They tapped on my door but I was from home. That sour semi-Scottish colleague tells me, as merrily as he can, that the FBI are Irish and thick, but they're thorough. He knows that I know that it isn't true that the FBI are all Irish. They may be thick, they certainly are thorough: and one morning on the way to college I am halted by a polite, alert, most unthick young man who shows me a picture and asks me have I ever seen that face.

No, it is no face that I've ever seen, that mock-up of the face of a sad man whose path nearly crossed mine (1968) and who (1977) breaks out for a weekend in the Tennessee mountains to brighten the monotony of ninety-nine years. Looking ahead at ninety-nine years is inclined to make a man restless. No, I tell the alert, unthick, polite young man, I never saw that face. I was away in holy Ireland (where such things don't happen) when the dreadful thing happened. We talk for a bit about Ireland. His origins are Italian so he knows all about it.

To one of the mustering places I go on the day of the funeral with the best intentions of walking all the way with the throng behind the farm wagon. But the long travelling in the heat beat me and I'm glad to crawl home and sit in an air-conditioned room and follow the sad spectacle on television.

The sound of the hunt fades away to the north, to Canada, then across the sea to Portugal and across the narrow seas to London. Had James Earl Ray enough money to pay his own fare all the way? Does petty robbery by one lone man pay off so well? The chase ends in the stereotyped, classical fashion with the Scotland Yard man saying: 'Excuse me sir, could you step aside here for a moment?' A sad, pathetic, hunted creature all his life, only to be rescued from utter oblivion by a deed of hate: and over the weekend that man was abroad in the Tennessee mountains. I looked again at two photographs of the boy that was to grow into the man that on TV the other evening one saw trudging, like a haltered animal, back to his eternal prison.

One photograph was taken when he was just turned ten and small for his age, in Ewing School in Ewing, Missouri. He is the last boy in the third row, a tiny fellow, barely visible, with tousled hair and a wide smile. Beside him stands his pal, Robey Peacock, a tall thin morose devil. They could only have been a comic couple when they moved about together. In the other picture he is fourteen years of age. He is snapped with three other people in front of a filling station. He wears a white sweater and looks happy. Beside him, as tall as giraffe or a peacock, is Robey Peacock, all legs, little torso. Robey died young.

Behind the little boy is a shiftless, petty criminal background. His father is reported to have said, and it sounds like a pitiable effort to brag, 'I don't know what the FBI got in mind for us. I think they intend to get rid of the whole Ray outfit, if you ask me. Sooner or later, shut us all up. That's what they're going for, if you ask me.' Would the poor man be heartened to know that one of them was to acquire distinction by murdering one of the best men of his time?

The pictures are in *An American Death* by Gerald Frank which, in so far as it relates to Ray, is the saddest American tragedy I've ever read of: no style here, no real villainy, Theodore Dreiser in reverse. Somewhere in the middle of the book his previous efforts at jailbreaks are recorded, each of them ending arse over tip. Considering the record an American lawyer, Robert K. Dwyer, is reported as saying, 'The man was never spared any humiliation.' Captured by blood hounds, plastered with mountain mud, he stumbles back into eternity.

DESMOND HOGAN
Without a Home (1987)

'Beauty's only skin deep but black is as deep as bone.' We were travelling through Alabama on a Greyhound Bus. The speaker of the rich observation reclined at the back of the bus. Sometimes he broke into song. Songs that sounded like spirituals. Maybe they were spirituals made up. And among the songs there was a story he was telling himself or the other passengers, a fragmentary but onward pressing sequence among the snatches of song. You could pick up words, phrases, episodes for a moment. 'Jail house.' 'Judge woman.' An image of fishing boats with lamps in them on the sea, and the sea being blessed from one of the boats by a priest. The middle-aged black man uttered what sounded like a prayer in Latin, a rasping and suddenly high-pitched benediction. All his words in fact, either quiet or suddenly loud and climactic, were suffused in a rich, nasal intonation. Outside the December light was golden, the fields looked bleached and demure. We passed through poor parts of small towns, black people were seated on the verandas, throwing glances at the bus, very often a Christmas tree beside them. From the suburbs of New Orleans onwards, in the gardens of more affluent homes, the

Nativity figures were sprinkled around in varying affiliations with one another. I'd bought a four weeks' Greyhound Bus pass in London for £132 and I'd set out from New Orleans, heading to places in the southern states where I'd always wanted to go. San Francisco was to be my Christmas venue after these places were experienced.

The garden district of New Orleans was quiet in early December, expectant. Blond boys breaking the emptiness of a street by cutting from one pub to another, with a quickness, as if the light hurt. Carmine rosettes were placed under the poinsettia pots on balconies, the American flag dripping everywhere from these white French and Spanish colonial houses. Houses that seemed to breathe their European ancestry, that seemed to exchange, to signal data to one another about the countries that inspired them. Marilyn Monroe was whole-heartedly mourned by Elton John from street-corner boutiques, from pubs, from shops which sold everything for cats, congestions of furry white mice. 'Candle in the Wind'. Elton John's words would suddenly and urgently break into your thoughts.

I'd always wanted to go to Columbus, Georgia. It would be like repaying a debt for the beauty of Carson McCullers's books. Elizabeth Bowen called her 'the child genius'. She was the poet of the universal small town boulevard, loved by those who knew the solitary red bar-light that slashed an empty night-time small-town street, the hieroglyphic wound of this light. She was the man-woman, her cheekbones on one photograph almost shading her face, her eyes alarmed, and a white, man's shirt sweeping the under-nourished bird-shoulders.

The bus stopped for a few hours in Montgomery, Alabama. Life for miles around seemed to presage on the Greyhound Bus station – people leave-taking or arriving, for the long streets were vacuous-looking in their furthest reaches and the far vistas of them were granted little activity. Twilight was burdensome like a summer twilight. It seemed to worry people, make them uneasy in their dealings with one another. The man in the canteen was parsimonious with the string beans.

I got into Columbus, Georgia, about ten at night, finding myself in a bus station which was thronged by young soldiers in brown shirts. A pool of sleepy eyes looked up at a stranger, pinning you for a moment with adolescent, dreamtime interest. (There is an important army camp near Columbus.) Carson McCullers had married one of the adolescent soldiers. Reeves McCullers. She'd made adolescent soldiers into non-combative, often exceedingly gentle fictional creatures. There is a world of soldiers in brown shirts in her books – young husbands, young lovers, fellow travellers. Her husband's travels ended in Paris where he killed himself, no longer a young soldier. She'd divorced him, married him again after he'd distinguished himself on Omaha Beach. There were many travels. One time, without her knowing it, he hid in the boat going to Europe which she was on. There was a house near Paris with a flourishing garden. There were literary postulations in Rome. But something, which had begun in innocence and which had infused itself into her fiction, ended in Paris. She refused to pay for his body to be returned from Europe so he was buried in Paris. Truman Capote said the day Reeves McCullers died was the day his youth ended. 'Il est mort stoiquement.' They would always be at best, in the way they looked in photographs near-adolescent lovers. And she contined to look like a near-adolescent, despite the paralysis of one side of her body, almost to the day she died, a kind of black beetle in standing, with an artichoke face. Her first stroke had happened before she was thirty.

Within a few minutes I was on that main street. I walked, mesmerised. A draper's shop window could have been a draper's shop window in Cahirciveen, County Kerry; the fifties feel, the ornate and almost over-demanding arrangements of garments, the peeling cowslip-colour paint on the windows. There was the business of finding a place to stay. The YMCA was full. So I stayed in the Heart of Columbus Motel, a motel with a rouge neon heart over it. The connection with the title of one of Carson McCullers's books was coincidental but maybe the word was an obsessive word in Columbus – like the word elder or drugstore, it had wagered its way into the young imagination of Carson McCullers.

Back on the main street I tried Blair's Bar for a drink. A cabin of a pub. I'd seen men playing pool through the window. 'A glass of white wine,' I asked for. 'We've none of the hard stuff,' the proprietress almost shrieked at me. I moved on. Past a cinema which was lighted up. I looked towards the foyer. Two young men stood outside. 'You're too old,' I though I heard them say. Apparently there was a teenagers' hop going on inside. In Davis's Bar I was given the nearest thing to wine. A bottle of Mountain Cooler. A taste of grapes somewhere in the gin-like substance. Few people stood on or walked on the street, there was a noiselessness from the cinema and you could see no one go in or go out which made the promise of the dance seem almost fake, an excuse for the two phantom boys outside.

The street in the morning sunshine was altogether different. The annual Christmas parade was happening. Carson McCullers lived away from Columbus, Georgia, for twenty-five years. She returned to renew her 'sense of horror'. An old black woman, red kerchief around her head and grey curls coming out from underneath it, talked to herself, hypnotised by her own talk, her back to a street corner, as the parade passed. A man had what appeared to be a balletic-looking epileptic fit on the other side of the street. On the bridge over the Chatahoochee – the other (Phoenix) side of the river being a different city – a jovial-looking man played a tune on a Prince Albert tobacco tin, interrrupting his playing to call out seasonal greetings. The trees in the distance by the river were still auburn, or was the colour a niggling russet in the sunshine? Healthy women were hoisted by, standing on the front of cars. Miss This. Miss That. A more sober and taciturn and even worried-looking Mrs Wives of America. Then there were the high-school majors and majorettes with their batons, the body-exultant cheerleaders. A whole troupe of demons in scarlet, long, springy tails on them, one white face among the black.

I slipped away from the parade to renew my search for Carson McCullers. 'Carson McCullers. Who?' Despite the girl's ignorance I did find a small glass case of memorabilia in the library, radically depleted for a symposium on McCullers in a nearby university. Anyway the small church halls along the way, the vast and seemingly disused mill with the meanderings of little railway tracks around it, were testimony. I thought of all the cotton-mill workers who crawled in for night-time coffees in her fiction, possibly to be assailed by a bit of a tramp's wisdom, a nugget, an inspiration from the roads. 1250 Starke Avenue was where she had lived, where she married Reeves McCullers. The reception was held in the back garden. A black dog jumped out from a radiant clump of pampas grass in the same garden when I was trying to conjure the wedding scene, stand-ing at a low fence, and chased me down the leafy suburban boulevard. But not before I'd got the chance to study the halldoor where the ingenuous child had performed plays, on the small verandah there, with the help of the sliding doors. Later in life she made the money that kept her to the end of her days from her stage adaptation of her novel, *The Members of the Wedding*, a play which featured little androgynous creatures with foggy male-female voices who might have been the ones drawn to the glamour of that halldoor once.

I had my hair cut by an old black man in a barber's shop on the main street and purchased a brown soldier's shirt in a thrift store. The bus wound on through the night to Ashville, North Carolina. 'The best thing is understanding between two people,' the black man had declared on the bus in Alabama. Carson McCullers's fiction had fought for, had even torn for, a description of that understanding, however briefly the understanding lasted.

*

'Something has spoken to me in the night, and told me to lift up my heart again and have no fear, and told me I shall live and work and draw my breath in quietness again and told me I shall die, I know not where.' Thomas Wolfe had written those lines in a Copenhagen hotel in 1935 in a moment of extreme self-doubt, lines that were later to be reworked into what was published as the end of *You Can't Go Home Again*. He had a couple of years to live, to build up a mess of manuscripts which other people had to decipher. The sudden mountainous freshness in the air told you you were were going into the Appalachians. That very freshness, that zest seemed a language in itself. We arrived in Ashville at six in the morning, nothing open near the station but Dunkin Donuts. The station was a few miles from the centre of town. A tramp who might have been one of Carson McCullers's tramps put his things in a locker without actually closing it, then changed his mind, took them out, put them in another locker, changed his mind again, kept going until he had tried every vacant locker. The tramp and I waited in Dunkin Donuts until first light, the tramp asking me for some small change and purchasing a doughtnut, with funereal purple icing on it, which he meditated on for a long time before eating. 'A man can't go back home again . . . I could never go back there to live, back there or any other place for long. I have to move. My home is in my work now.'

After getting a room in a motel I walked around town. It was the annual Christmas party at the Thomas Wolfe Memorial, the house Wolfe and his family had moved into from another house in Ashville when he was a child, and you were welcomed at the door with warm cider. A woman was playing 'The Mountains of Mourne' on the piano. Scenes from Thomas Wolfe's fiction seemed to rush at you from the rooms so resonant were they of his time, his work. A copy of *A Daughter of the Highlanders* lying about in an upstairs room, the sound of Edwardian tunes coming from below, even an ancient and Atlantic-liner-looking lavatory bowl had poignance.

I walked to Riverside cemetery where he was buried. It sloped down to a view of the Appalachians. Afternoon light was amber. I paid homage by kneeling in front of the grave. 'Death bent to touch his chosen son with mercy, love, and pity, and put the seal of honour on him when he died.' I suddenly became aware of two youths standing quite still nearby, surveying me. With their casual jackets, the overweening pair of glasses on one of them, they looked like college students. 'Did you know that O. Henry is buried here too? He's a better writer.' My eye seemed to catch successfully a grave-stone with the name Henry on it. 'Not there. O. Henry's real name was William Porter.' My ignorance disgusted them and they went off, disappearing among the grave-stones.

Sunday was silent in Ashville, North Carolina. On the publication of the recent biography a leading American newspaper dismissed Wolfe, the voluptuousness and sometimes baby-prattle dementia of his prose, saying he no longer needed to be considered in the canon of American literature. The air at Riverside cemetery said differently, the staleness, the greyness of the Sunday streets in Ashville. He and Carson McCullers had caught the loneliness of the small town and the spirit that keeps trying, no matter how defeated it feels at times, to fight its way out. Much further on in my travels, in Wyoming, my fellow passengers and myself found ourselves stranded when the bus halted in the snow one night. Rescued by the Red Cross, I lay down on a school gymnasium floor for the night. I felt much safer here than I did in an ever-more-oppressive London. 'You speak American real good,' a very heavy woman on crutches had told me in Chicago when we were stuck there for thirty-six hours because of the snow, a woman who summarily collapsed in the bus station and was taken to hospital. She'd been on her way to her native Iowa City for treatment, a place she hadn't visited for twenty years, abandoned to the journey in Knoxville, Tennessee, by her son and husband, a nefarious pair who'd come to send her off with crutches and two huge cases. Such stories are part of the ultimate kaleidoscope, as are the desultory images, while you wait in bus stations during blizzards – a little black boy playing with a toy Greyhound Bus, a bus you can put coins in. The toy, the way it's upheld, seems to hold your fate for a moment, this innocent object to have the power to decide the fluctuations of your voyage, the snowstorms, the panoramic vistas, the companions, the chance conversations that may lead to further meetings in cities in another continent.

On our way again, on a snowy night, as the bus descended into California, people, one group or one individual after another, sang 'Silent Night' in their own language. There were Cubans, German-Swiss, English, French, a Ukranian survivor of a German concentration camp. A plump girl didn't join in any of the excitement between performances. She stared ahead. An orphan since birth, she was on her way from New York to San Francisco looking for a waitressing job. A little Cuban man in a fawn coat and his impeccably groomed children, two boys and two girls, were making a similar move to Sacramento. All his children were in fawn coats too, the girls with bountiful bows in their red ribbons. Before the songs, he had passed over a succession of cherished family photographs to me, which he produced one by one from a briefcase, no wife in any of the photographs. A sixteen-year-old Swiss punk had run away from Basel, lots of chains on him, his pale knee judiciously exposed by a tear in his greasy trousers, his hair black prongs that stuck up over a ewe-delicate face that kept breaking into an ethereally appreciative smile. In Basel his wife's lover used to beat him up. A Hispanic gay in glittering shirt and trousers was the most theatrical of the singers, standing up, hands outstretched as he delivered 'Silent Night'. An aristocratic Englishwoman was exiled from England for some reason. She seemed to brood a lot between the urgent conversations she had with people. Anyway I'd told her that her home country had changed. For lots of us it was the same story; we couldn't go home again.

SEAMUS HEANEY

New Worlds

In the country poetry has deserted
Things fall in place like the plate-glass doors in banks.

There is a great calm.
The preserved churches are cool at noon

The good life hums and clinks in sidewalk cafés
Along the quays of sun-fed old canals.

Satiety in that air
Is so consistent and unostentatious

The sated traveller returns for more,
Grateful that his privilege is condoned.

In the country poetry has deserted,
In a language tonic as their swimming pools,

There are many poets, all insisting
Their poetry brings new worlds into being.

RICHARD MURPHY

Sri Lanka

Being nearly heart-shaped made me seem a ham
    On early spice trade navigators' charts
    Tinctured with cinnamon, peppered with forts,
To be eaten up under a strong brand name
Like Taprobane, Serendib, Tenarisim —
    Copper-palmed lotus island slave resorts —
    And I succumbed to lordly polished arts
That cut me down to seem a white king's gem,
A star sapphire tear-drop India shed
    On old school maps, a lighthouse of retorts
Flashing from head to head. My leonine blood
Throbbed wildly when resplendent freedom came
Mouthing pearl tropes with Pali counterparts,
Exalted, flawed; and made me seem as I am.

DEREK MAHON
(*Two Poems after Philippe Jaccottet*)

The Voice

What is it that sings when the other voices are silent?
Whose is that pure, deaf voice, that sibilant song?
Is it down the road on a snow-covered lawn
or close at hand, aware of an audience?
This is the mysterious first bird of dawn.
Do you hear the voice increase in volume
and, as a March wind quickens the creaking trees,
sing mildly to us without fear,
content in the fact of death? Do you hear?
What does it sing in the grey dawn? Nobody knows;
but the voice is audible only to those
whose hearts are emptied of property and desire.

Ignorance

The older I get the more ignorant I become;
the longer I live the less I possess or control.
All I have is a little space, snow-dark
or glittering – never inhabited.
Where is the giver, the guide, the guardian?
I sit in my room and am silent. Silence
comes in like a servant to tidy things up
while I wait for the lies to disperse.
And what remains to this dying man
that so well prevents him from dying?
What does he find to say to the four walls?
I hear him talking still, and his words
come in with the dawn, imperfectly formed:
'Love, like fire, can only reveal its clarity
on the failure and the beauty of ashen forests.'

MONGANE WALLY SEROTE

An Interview

Could you tell me about your childhood?

I was born in Sophiatown, in 1944. About four years after that we moved to Alexandria, which is also in Johannesburg, and I went to school near Alexandria, and also in Lesotho, Soweto and the USA. Eventually I did what they call a Master of Fine Arts in the US. I started writing, I think, when I was about fourteen. I think why I started writing at that age was that, for some reason or other, I was reading a lot at that stage and I don't know if this is hindsight or what but I think when one reads a lot and comes from Alexandria you realise that most of the things that you read don't have anything to do with the life that you lead. At this stage I really felt that I could write about my life as I knew it. The strange thing is that I'm sure because reading for me was based on anything that I came across and most of it was thrillers and things like that I started writing in the form of thrillers but then stopped because at the school in Lesotho they told me I was wasting my time. Subsequently, for some reason or other, I don't know why, I started writing poetry if one can call it poetry. I don't know what it was I was writing, but it was what I thought was poetry. I don't have material from that time.

After high school, I started journalism, which means I was sort of apprenticed to one of the popular newspapers. This put me in contact with a wide range of people throughout the country and I began to understand what was happening in South Africa. The first thing that really strikes one about South Africa, if you are doing journalism and doing it in the sections I was doing it in, is that there is very extreme and abject poverty. But when one is aware of this one is also aware that there are also people who are very very wealthy, and the demarcation is really colour of skin. You begin to understand that whites are very very rich and blacks are very very poor.

Being black means at one level being threatened all the time by poverty, by ignorance, by illiteracy, and as you grow other things begin to become very real for one. For instance you realise that by virtue of being what you are, you are always liable to become a prisoner. The streets that one walks are extremely dangerous in the sense that from a very early age it had become normal for us to know that people can get killed in the streets by hooligans, to start with, and also by the police. I think at a certain point all these things combine.

On one level they begin to make one doubt oneself as to the significance of being alive at all. On the other you feel you have been wronged to use a very mild word indeed. And throughout you try to resolve the contradiction: what is the meaning of this? One can deal with it in that sense if one can become abstract, but things in South Africa are not abstract. The police come into the locations, the townships, and you begin to understand that they have absolutely no respect and at the same time you understand that they are supposed to be representing law and order. And then of course you hear from your parents about how their lives have been; you see what happens to them when you travel with them or go with them into town and you begin to understand that in fact your being alive is really considered a crime.

I'm saying all this to say that it's not possible for me to pinpoint how one becomes a writer, and takes writing as seriously as I do, and takes what is happening in South Africa as seriously as I do. But amidst all this confusion there is one very significant thing which, as one grows older, one begins to understand in its significance, and to read why it is necessary to be hopeful about life.

Can you tell us something about your genesis as a writer?

After the events of 1960, especially after Sharpeville where sixty-seven people were killed by the apartheid regime, after that the regime really went all out to wipe out our history, by killing people, by putting them into long terms of imprisonment, by making them scuttle into exile, through banning orders, house arrests, banishments and also through banning of whatever species of writing had come out of that experience before the sixties. So really we were a generation that had to search very very desperately indeed for who we were, where we were going, where we come from; which I think at a certain point explains the birth of what came to be called 'the Black Consciousness era'.

It started first of all among students, which means that students for the first time had access to international knowledge and as a result must have come across information regarding our history, and, as a way of rebelling and protesting against what had happened to us as a people, started a movement, but of course it was a movement that didn't take the history of struggle into consideration. I'm not blaming the people who were the spear-headers of this movement, I'm just saying that they were starting as if it was on a blank sheet, whereas it was not so. Hence the name of 'Black Consciousness'. It is important to view Black Consciousness very positively, because while at one side it was polarising people by colours of skin, it did mean that blacks could look at themselves as people, not as negatives of other people, and could assert themselves, especially the young people. It was very important that we did so because we were coming out of a vacuum, where all our leaders were absent.

We had to assert ourselves, we had to search for a history of struggle, we had to search for a direction. In that sense Black Consciousness was very positive. It did a whole lot for us to do certain things which other people in other countries take for granted: to understand that one doesn't owe anything to anybody because one is alive, that I am black is not a problem, etc. It was very important that this happened. The only problem starts after the young people discover that they have a very long history of struggle. Then they want to disassociate themselves from that and that becomes a problem. For those young people who have acknowledged our history of struggle, acknowledged our leaders, acknowledged our very old and very experienced organisation, the ANC, I think there is a point of departure.

Of course now we are talking a different language. Too many people have been killed, expecially young men and young women, little children. Too many will continue to be killed. But slaves arrive at a point where they realise that death is a liberator. Another important fact has been found through active struggle: that it has become necessary not only to die for freedom but also to kill for freedom – very unfortunate discoveries. If people arrive at that I think all of us will agree that it is because the situation has developed to the worst it can.

We have been told a lot about the West: the West has been a pioneer of civilisation over many years and the West had given us no choice but to refer to it for civilisation and progress. As a people thrown into oblivion, into that dark part of history, we have told the world in no uncertain terms that that condition is completely unacceptable to us. And of course the first people we appeal to are the civilised people who we expect to be the first to understand that there is no person who will accept the conditions we are living in. The situation as it is now tells us that civilisation was for white people only.

Whatever the Western countries may have said about us, in a nutshell this is what it comes to. When we say we are not prepared to accept white domination, we are not prepared to accept relegation into backyards of history, it seems the West cannot understand what we are talking about. Of course you can choose to be bewildered by this. We are not, I don't think we should be bewildered at all.

Right now everybody talks about a bloodbath. Privately one wonders how it is possible for the world to talk about a bloodbath with such great familiarity and acceptance when the world has gone through two world wars. How is it that Western governments can talk with such ease in terms of accepting a bloodbath? One privately thinks about this and always hopes that the people in the West will read correctly the real meaning of the bloodbath and ask themselves if they would like this to happen. On the other hand, for us we either accept the full meaning of a bloodbath and live through it, or we accept something that nobody will ever accept voluntarily: that we must remain an oppressed, exploited people. It is understandable that the choice is very, very difficult, but the events as they unfold in South Africa show that, as a people, we have accepted the consequences of all that.

As a writer, this is what is constantly in one's mind. What do I do with this knowledge? Of course at a certain level it becomes intolerable to always to have to deal with such grim issues on a daily basis twenty-four hours but at the same time I don't think one regrets being alive at this point. Both as a person and a writer I have learnt how far, how deep, hope can be. I think I'm much richer because of that knowledge. I realise that knowledge has been extremely expensive in terms of my people, but that is what I've inherited. I've also come to understand the meaning of optimism, in its fullest sense, and because of this I am aware that very little will shock me after this. And all this is a point of reference for my writing. It is very important for me that I create a proper – if one can be as arrogant as that – a proper point of reference for my people as a writer, I hope I'm capable of that. But also for people generally in the world. Now that is being very ambitious, but one can only say that precisely because one has experienced as an individual and belonging to a people who have gone through what they have, one has experienced this very deep wealth which the world has forgotten, because I'm sure it knows this: it is not possible the world should have gone through two world wars and not know what the people of South Africa are experiencing now. So one wonders how does one remind the whole world about this.

One feels one should use one's time in Europe now to fully understand the experience of Europeans: what they have inherited from the two world wars, what it means to them, and in whatever small way one can contribute to make this world a better place in which to live. When one is in Europe one realises how much life is threatened. One listens to Reagan, to Kohl in Germany, and one realises that these people command such power that if one is not careful one can feel extremely insignificant and minute. But again, one begins to understand another thing when one is in Europe, that people, and here I'm talking about ordinary people like anybody else in the world, will not accept being subjected to blackmail throughout their lives. If governments subject their people to poverty, unemployment, threat of war, people will not accept this. One begins to see a commonness between what is happening in South Africa and what is happening in Europe. One can sense the impending danger that the world is facing, but one also begins to understand, to size up, the hope that people have about their lives. This has also become a point of reference, to deal with a human dilemma as we live it in 1986.

You have also spent some months in prison. I imagine this was also a fundamental experience for you.

I was arrested in June 1969 and I was released in February 1970. All I can say about that is that I don't wish anybody to experience that. But you see, people do experience it, which means it is something we have to face very squarely. During that nine months one was in solitary confinement. One had been told in no uncertain terms that one would see nobody else but the security branch.

Those two things are the cruellest things: to keep somebody in solitary confinement for a full nine months and tell that person he will be there indefinitely and nobody else will see him. About that there was very, very serious torture. You see, if you know that, if you have that information and it is part of your life, initially you become extremely angry when people debate as to whether it does happen or not. Of course it is very naive, but you'd have thought that nobody, under no circumstances, nobody's child, must be in that condition, people would believe what you say, but the world is not like that. The world has listened to the people who created that condition, the masters of torture, and the world has also listened to people who have been subjected to that very severe pain which changes your life completely.

To me it happened in 1969 and 1970. I still listen to debates about that. I know, when fourteen-year-old children come out of that and say they have been tortured, I know what they mean. All you have to do is to look at a person and you know it. But the world doesn't operate like that. As a result, thousands of people in South Africa are experiencing that daily. Under no circumstances should anybody's child be subjected to that.

Physical torture was extremely intense. I never thought a human being could go to that level, but I saw them do it and they are free men even now: they drive cars, they sleep with their wives, they talk to their children, even now, extremely cruel people, very cruel people. I still read about them in the newspapers. I'm talking about a long time ago in terms of time, but it's a thing I will never forget, I can't forget.

Just the other day a chief interrogator, a man called Sonapool, gave an interview to the *Guardian* here. There he is, the man owns a farm, he says he's a 'rainmaker' on a daily basis, when he wakes up he puts a pistol on his hip and walks around his farm and I'm sure he's working with many black farm labourers, he still has his wife and children and everybody. He was saying that what is happening now could have been stopped in 1976 if some of the politicians, some of the police, were not cowards. They were cowards because they were afraid to kill. He said, 'When I led a riot squad, I killed mercilessly when I went to the townships' and says the only solution to the South African problem is that.

Now I was face to face with this man seven days and seven nights: he doesn't surprise me when he says that. In a sense that man is an actual embodiment of apartheid. That is what apartheid is all about. I'll tell you a very sad story. During one of the sessions of interrogation he came to me and said, 'The woman that you so respected,' he was talking about a very close friend of mine, a woman who taught me a whole lot of things – 'we've reduced her to a point where she has been menstruating for the past week non-stop.' At that time I hadn't addressed what menstruation meant in that context, but it was very grim information for me, to think what could have happened. And as he was saying this, that man was drinking coffee. I did not believe what he said, I was sure it was just a tactic to try and push me, but when I met my friend she told me it was true, they had pushed her so much. A man who could sit, drink coffee and say a thing like that and be given so much power, it just shows how much that country has gone mad. A complete madness.

Another information is that in '69 we were among the first people to be detained under the Terrorism Act, Section 6. Before that they were detaining mainly people from rural areas and people from Namibia and they were very quiet about it, which means they were killing many people. It so happened that while we were detained there was a case on about a man called Lingwe who was killed during torture. This man came to me and said, 'I'm sure before we came to take you from home you were reading about Lingwe. I'll tell you how we killed him.' He was standing there, walking up and down, while his colleagues were laughing. On one side that is information coming from that nine months, but there is also a physical part which one can only describe with a very weak word, torture. And you know, as we are sitting here, we are told over two thousand people have been detained. For me, when that is said, one has to consciously keep balance, because I know exactly what is going on. The world has reduced this to a figure on paper 2000 but for me it's not and for many people it cannot be. This is why I say, in Europe, where are the people who were there during the Second World War, what do they say when they hear this information? Some of them are in government, and some of them went through that, which says something very bad about human beings. For me, constantly, I ask myself where are these people who know what this means and who have allowed the world the reduce it to four figures?

AUSTIN CLARKE

The Gate
(*from* The House of Terror)

The mind is often as much affected by the house in which the body
dwells as by the house that is not built with hands. The ancestral
house now falling to ruin with its rich dim traditions of age, the
castles at Radcliffe with strange dungeons and instruments of torture,
the house of childhood, in which lost empty room or attic affects the
child before sleep with strange and terrible fascination, the haunted
house which seems living and peopled to the dreamer. There is
something as of personality in all these.

But in an institution, a workhouse, a prison, a madhouse by which
civilisation is most rapidly perceived, there is [a] lack of such, an
impersonal quality, that discipline of bars [,] insurmountable stone
walls. Of these three the last is the most interesting as much from
itself as from the customs of its unrented occupiers. It becomes one's
own world, but a silent unreceptive microcosm. It has the silent resistance of the prison, yet a little more colour. Because one is aware of
it, knowing but the past, it seems vast, ominous. Glimpses of lost
rooms, of small closets, unlocked for a moment, fill the imagination
as of a child who penetrates some lost room. The long rows of locked
doors with a small observation window, seem like cells, or perhaps
vaults, enriched with white paint by some mad humour. It would be
indeed untrue to call it merely the House of Terror, but there is
something in madness, not simple as tragedy, but mixed. Something
that is akin to melodrama, superficially seen, for there, tears and joy
are mixed without incongruity. It is a world, a complete humanity in
itself, a herded humanity as indeed the same outside, one where the
actors seemed compelled to speak the lines given to them by the
dramatists, but where more than in real life, the great simple
passions, rage, joy, despair, the unmixed material of dreams, yet all
moved by some force in common, as outside a populace is moved by
politics or creeds, and by what is the most common and precious –
reason; but here by a power that has profound reason mixed with the
[?its] absence. Not though a House of Terror, for I have met the
happiest men in all the world inside the mad house in which I resided.

But to some who have not reached the desirable impersonality of hopeless madness, it might well be so. I therefore set down without theory or partiality, my experiences, accepting the rich contrasts of life and society, having no wishes to reform, neither regret nor grievance.

If I have seen agony, I have perhaps also known it and accept it as a part of life. It will be found that many of the colloquial references to madness are humourous, such represent the wisdom of ages and perhaps represent some truth of which I reminisce. Yet by a sudden reversion of attitude, the fantastic gesture of [the mad] seemed as natural as the lack of reflex actions or uniformity of that which is the most obvious sign of sanity. Cerebral disease merely, I do not write of, but rather of the infirmity of imagination in which will and mind are not all compact. To most, lunacy has a dull uniformity to be hidden away. Commonsense is as material or founded as the feeling of existence, unperceived as the perfect digestion.

In this case I show the feeling of terror, flooding and breaking down the soul of the individual. Much I have indeed forgotten, or have been oblivious to, subliminal states apprehended yet like the tail of a disappearing dream untroubled of language, but certain [;] states, that vivid, light up as much of the darkness and those lurid [;] perhaps the light itself is madness, my sole subject, of the intensified keenness of observation in madness as we say 'cunning as a madman' help in this, of this more later.

To me that state was one of highlights and shadows, as in deliriums or a torpor [,] beautiful happy nirvana of which little can be said. The happiness of the vegetation [,] and words could not exaggerate.

The Gate is an unseen but dominant reality. It is a word used regularly. It to me assumed the terms of the Gates of the Inferno of Dante. It meant eternal imprisonment, the abandonment of hope which the criminal has, no counting of days or of years. Howley, a young solicitor, with handsome distainful features, said to have been a student of the priesthood once, ending I know not how, is a proud madness. He strode up and down always addressing: 'Give me my boots please and let me out of the Gate and to pleasant jest, dogs, hogs, workhouse tramps and paupers,' and nameless obscenities. Perhaps even addressing menials in his cultured voice politely requesting and then ending in curses. But those distinct images never give answers. The world in city lies beyond us. One would hear lost murmuring, but of that busy life of lit shops and the theatres and crowds, few I imagine knew. It is something remote, abstract.

As I travelled at a rapid pace, the mind increased by that speed, the lights in the fog or a glimpse of black waters, a curious acuteness to impression, we paused and I heard the sound of gates closing. A curious intuition of this place, gleaming of trees and wet gravel in the lamplight. Afterwards I remembered that when I was a child, an accident, crowds, I had been here, gates by some church opened and I strayed with that curious fear of a child doing wrong. So deep are the impressions of childhood.

A Commentary by Dardis Clarke

It has been public knowledge for years that the poet Austin Clarke (1896-1974) spent some time in Saint Patrick's Hospital, Dublin, following a nervous breakdown. His long poem *Mnemosyne Lay in Dust* (1966) drew on this experience, and in doing so incorporated some shorter poems written earlier. However, just after he left the hospital founded on money left by Johnathan Swift, Clarke composed a prose account of his stay there. Entitled *The House of Terror*, and written probably in 1920, it has been never been published. The manuscript was written in the author's small hand-writing, with letters unjoined; as far as is known, no typed version was ever prepared. The manuscript runs to thirty-seven pages, and the extract published above constitutes the first chapter, 'The Gate'.

The manuscript has the status of an authorial draft, at times resembling a memorandum addressed to the author himself. Consequently, one cannot find in it the consistency of punctuation, or evenly-paced argument, of a finished typescript. Yet it is obvious that the poet referred to it more than forty five-years later when he came to put down his experiences in the verse of *Mnemosyne Lay in Dust*. Something of his compositional method can be gauged from a comparison of the two passages which follow; first the prose of 1920:

> Cyclops seized me, white gleam of beds, of strange faces passed. I was flung into darkness and I heard the sound of heavy bolts. I lay on the cold ground for an endless period

too terrified to move, aware only of my breathing. At last I groped around feeling with my hands a circular wall. There was no opening. I was suffocating. I would choke. I called aloud, imploring, but my voice was a whisper. I beat the walls and my knuckles pained, but there was only a dull sound. I rushed around like an animal frenzied, suffocating. Nothing but silence. Exhausted I lay there and as I scratched at what seemed the floor a terrible intuition filled me. I was in a padded cell.

And here, with its third-person narrative, is the third stanza from Section VI of the poem:

He tumbled into half the truth:
Burial alive. His breath was shouting:
'Let, let me out.' But words were puny.
Fists hushed on a wall of inward-outness.
Knees crept along a floor that stirred
As softly. All was the same chill.
He knew the wall was circular
And air was catchcry in the stillness
For reason had returned to tell him
That he was in a padded cell.

AGNES NEMES NAGY
(translated from Hungarian by Hugh Maxton)

Lazarus

Round his left shoulder, as he got up slowly
every day's muscle gathered in agony.
His death was flayed off him, like a gauze.
Because second-birth has just such harsh laws.

The Sleeping Form

Unknown and naked,
you rise from ash.
You are in the seventh room,
not dead, only sleeping.

Only sleeping, bed of whittles,
between the ashen walls,
the wrecked curtain gives the silence
huge motionless wings.

I do not move.
Only, like slowly tumbling sheaves,
only your visions in their courses
move, like black stars.

Wake, wake up. Uncover that shoulder.
Wounded or not. I will find you.
Talk that I may talk till death.
Speak, speak finally wherever
in your mute dream.

W. J. Mc CORMACK

Communicating with Prisoners

> Sea-borne, or balanced on the air
> When first it sprang out of the nest
> Upon some lofty rock to stare
> Upon the cloudy canopy,
> While under its storm-beaten breast
> Cried out the hollows of the sea.
>
> W. B. Yeats

In the Sligo County Library and Museum, there is a painting by Jack Butler Yeats entitled 'Communicating with Prisoners'. Dating from 1924, it is an exact contemporary of Ernst Toller's German Expressionist play, *The Swallow Book*, which shares some of its thematic concerns. The right-hand side of the picture is dominated by a blue-grey tower with a row of small square windows near the top framing some shadowy figures: these look down (if indeed they can see anything) over an urban skyline. Here is, then, no Willyeatsian tower or rural antique restored on the proceeds of lecture tours and surplus Nobel funds. It is a grim, functional, contemporary jail; virtually architecture-less, it has 'use value', not history. Yet the foreground shows seven women, hatted and eminently respectable; the line of these links the base of the tower to a flimsier structure on the left in the immediate foreground: a bill-board or hoarding, with posters advertising a bazaar and a sale clearly discernible. Mid-way up the hoarding, the lacy cuff of an elegant poster hand points inwards towards the tower, and above this cut-off theatrical figure there is a further poster in which a man's legs are seen climbing a ladder. (Is this the bill poster himself, an interior reference to the artist – the painter ascending to work, or the visionary withdrawing?) Jack Yeats's Civil War painting employs a conventional scene at the prison gates, and juxtaposes this with carnivalesque hints at life's potential for joy. Yet even the carnival includes an oblique acknowledgement of the ultimate sacrifice prisoners might be forced to make for their cause, at the top of the gallow's ladder.

Women are so often seen as the patient figures who wait outside the prison gates that some redress of the balance is called for locally. Two Irishwomen occupying very different stations in life come to mind. The novelist Maria Edgeworth, child of the Enlightenment and eventually a landowner, accompanied her father to visit their publisher, Joseph Johnson, when he was imprisoned on a charge of sedition in 1799. Anne Devlin, a serving-girl, was illegally detained and tortured in Kilmainham in the wake of Robert Emmet's rebellion. In 1843 she was discovered living in penury by a historian; to him and to a Carmelite friar a secondary debt is owed by readers of her 'prison journal'. The Russian poet, Anna Akhmatova, who created a series of poems which re-enact this vigil at the prison gate, has no equivalent in Irish literature. On the contrary; when an imprisoned Irishwoman of elevated birth became the subject of a poem by W. B. Yeats, the result inaugurated a crisis of artistic conscience, a crisis in which neither art nor conscience distinguished itself. Subliminally, this forgotten episode may inform Seamus Heaney's sustained if necessarily retrospective interest in the poet-prisoners of Stalinism, notably Osip Mandelstam. And it has remained for a latter-day film director, Pat Murphy, to recognise the aesthetic power of Anne Devlin's now no longer neglected story.

There is a persistent Irish tradition which links the prison and the intellectual, however infrequently. The intention of the present paper is to examine a particular crisis within this tradition, and to consider briefly the implications in relation to the life of Nelson Mandela. In the eighteenth century, a sub-literature began to emerge in which speeches from the dock or last words from the gallows (real and invented) played an important part in shaping a particular notion of the prisoner's dilemma. From the case of Fr Nicholas Sheehy (1766) to that of Robert Emmet (1803), one can trace a growing exploitation of the printed medium to consolidate or deliberately to confuse. Emmet's fame is largely dependent on his *Speech from the Dock*, a version of which became a rhetorical performance from the late nineteenth century onwards. Yeats read a version of it aloud in February 1914, and as a schoolgirl Bernadette Devlin ranked it among her favourite recitations. Despite this latter-day renown, it is very difficult to establish what exactly Emmet said on 19 September 1803. Moreover, among early texts of his alleged speech one finds a version printed in the London-printed paper, *The Loyalist*, in October 1803. In these early instances, of course, the prisoner had been executed and no personal authentification was possible.

Political agitation throughout the nineteenth century saw fewer executions and the growth instead of penal servitude for life and occasional mass-transportation as means of control. As a result, prison literature expanded in bulk even if it lost immediacy. John Mitchel's *Jail Journal* (1854) provided a model for the later Fenian prisoners, John Devoy and John O'Leary, when they came to write their memoirs. The widespread appeal of this literary troupe can be gauged from two contrasting phenomena: the proto-socialist James Fintan Lalor worked on a newspaper deliberately named *The Irish Felon* – criminality in the eyes of others can enhance identity in one's own eyes – while the *symboliste* Yeats drew inspiration from both Mitchel and O'Leary. These nineteenth-century instances of prison literature relate, almost exclusively, to the nationalist cause. Nationalism was able to tap for its readers the deep emotional implications of the author's having written his book in, or only on release from, prison. Imprisonment was in this way doubly established as a bond of identity and as a palpable symbol of the oppression against which author and reader together stood. In this sense, the bondage which prisoners suffered could positively enhance bonding with their readers. When supporters of the status quo got so out of hand as to end up in jail – and sometimes they did! – no such powerful urge towards publication operated.

This distinction between the radical and conservative attitudes towards the possibilities of a prison literature can be observed in even more acute form at later periods of Irish history. Both Charles Stewart Parnell and Michael Davitt spent time in jail, under strikingly contrasting conditions it should be admitted; Parnell published nothing, the radical Davitt lived by his pen. Or, to skip ahead, we find that the principal beneficiary of the 1916 Rising (Eamon de Valera) abjured publication, whereas among those of his comrades who were executed were the poets Thomas Mc Donagh, Patrick Pearse, and Joseph Mary Plunkett, not to mention the socialist activist and writer, James Connolly. The larger context of the First World War may have conditioned the re-introduction of capital punishment, and certainly determined the use of the military firing squad as distinct from the gallows, symbol of offence against the civil order.

Imprisonment which led to execution (as in the case of the Easter

Rising poets) must appear as an exceptional incident in Irish literary history. Yet the case of Oscar Wilde in 1895-1897 deserves mention, as does the treatment meted out to suffragettes both British and Irish. The prisoner, whatever the reason for his/her imprisonment, was regarded sympathetically at a certain level of nationalist ideology. In the twentieth century, the coming together of prison and literature usually occurred in the context of nationalist/republican politics. The War of Independence, and Civil War, provided sensitive material for at least two excellent short story writers, Frank O'Connor and Sean O'Faolain, while the novelist Francis Stuart frequently incorporated scenes of imprisonment in his early novels, anticipations of the more extensively autobiographical work which followed his residence in Germany during the Second World War. Later, figures as contrasting as Brendan Behan and Ian Paisley have contributed to this prison literature.

*

The establishment of the Irish Free State in 1921 virtually coincided with the rise of fascism in continental Europe, and with the latter, the question of imprisonment took on a new and dreadful reality for intellectuals and political activists alike. To a large degree, the Irish pattern diverged from the European, and some account should be taken of this fact in assessing the reaction of Irish writers to events on the continent. For all the international renown of Irish writing in this period – the fame of W. B. Yeats, the notoriety of James Joyce – the traffic in cultural admiration was one-way, not mutual. Thus, victims of fascism who were silenced, exiled, tortured, hounded to death or simply murdered have names which strike many in the English-speaking world as intrusively new, even today. The name of the prisoner has a power to disturb.

It is agreed then that conditions in Europe in the 1930s, including penal conditions, differed yet surely not so markedly as to discredit all reports of fascist and (in time) Nazi brutality. One notable observer of European affairs, William Butler Yeats, had been awarded the Nobel Prize for Literature in 1923, in a ceremony which linked recognition both of his literary genius and the new independence of Ireland. Henceforth, in private and in public, he paid particular attention to political change – to Lenin and the Bolshevik experiment in the Soviet Union, Mussolini's fascist state in Italy, and the rise of Hitler. At home in Ireland in the twenties, he participated in the consolidation of the Free State during the Civil War, supported the use of flogging by the army, and defended the position of the once-great landowners. His rhetoric tended to associate these positions with civil liberties – the need to protect infant Independence on the one hand, to resist state censorship and Church-dominated moral codes on the other. But Yeats's personal relations with many of the participants in the independence movement underwent a more profound and contradictory crisis, a crisis in which the position of the prisoner as such took on new symbolic undertones.

To a considerable extent, Yeats's education as an Irish poet proceeded under the tutelege of ex-prisoners. In his earliest apprenticeship among the Fenians, John O'Leary was his chosen model of stoic endurance, even if he found O'Leary's *Recollections* (1896) dusty and dry compared to Mitchel's *Jail Journal*. Turning to London, he studied the conversational style and aesthetic discipline of Oscar Wilde, who a few years later composed (on location, so to speak) 'The Ballad of Reading Gaol'. Yeats remarked that Wilde was meant to be a man of action. Surely Wilde was closer to understanding the subject and perhaps foreseeing the Yeats of the 1930s when he observed that 'there is always something peculiarly impotent about the violence of a literary man . . . it is never kept in check by action.'

Jail-birds could appear in the most unlikely guises. In 1914 Yeats jointly staged a 'peacock dinner' in honour of Wilfrid Scawen Blunt, the minor English poet and ardent anti-imperialist. When Blunt had been jailed in Ireland in 1888, he composed a sonnet sequence *In Vinculis*; Wilde reviewed it favourably – in part at least because the occasion allowed him to assail Arthur Balfour who had also jailed William O'Brien. A man who could live up his name in describing people, Blunt found Yeats 'sleek and fat as becomes a prosperous man and one taking himself very seriously': that was in 1915, after one of Yeats's Emmet-invoking American tours.

But the great poems relied on unimpeachable historical fact. Like O'Leary, Emmet and Wolfe Tone in 'September 1913', all of the figures so ritually endorsed in 'Easter 1916' had been imprisoned at least once. Both Parnell and Casement, subjects of separate and strategically later poems, had been jailed, and again Casement had forfeited his life. Of the women who played so important a part in the poet's emotional development, certainly two had spent time inside, though here too the relatively late date at which they were still being incarcerated (January 1923 in the case of Maud Gonne Mac Bride, 1923-24 in that of Constance Markievicz) contributes to the difficulties Yeats experienced in confronting the issue of imprisonment.

The poem 'On a Political Prisoner', the last stanza of which is quoted as an epigraph above, was published in *The Dial* in November 1920, before the War of Independence was over. In 1918 Constance Markievicz had been imprisoned in Holloway Jail, London, while she held the position of Minister of Labour in the Irish underground government. (Later she was held in Mountjoy Jail, Dublin, and the city jail in Cork.) References to the Sligo landscape in the third stanza clearly indicate the biographical focus, and yet the distinctly impersonal title ('On' rather than 'To') introduces a poem which works steadily to distance the poet from the prisoner and, nevertheless, to re-assimilate her to a natural order which he believes had been disrupted by her radically democratic politics. The first stanza recounts how the prisoner fed a grey sea-gull through the bars of her cell window. In the second, the poet asks whether this renewed contact with nature recalled the years before her mind 'Became a bitter, an abstract thing.' In the third, he remembers her youth explicitly in terms of aristocratic recreations; by grammatical elision he identifes her with natural beauty *in extenso* (1.15), but then proceeds to emphasise the image of her isolation – 'Like any rock-bred, sea-borne bird . . . '. We then move to the last stanza in which the prisoner has been transformed into a natural being outside the prison bars, free yet willing to feed from the prisoner's hand.

Nature and politics are here juxtaposed in a manner familiar enough to readers of the conservative strain in modernist literature. Readers have been conditioned to prefer the former or, to examine the issue more precisely, a crude dichotomy of immediacy and abstraction has gone unchallenged within criticism of this literature. The poem in question, however, has distinctive features even if it cannot be said to rank exceptionally high in Yeats's *oeuvre*. 'She/her' occurs no less than ten times in the first eighteen lines, and appears nowhere in the remaining six lines as if to indicate that release was a release from gender. Feminists will have no difficulty making a point here, but a more precise transformation is the making possible (and yet witholding) a patient, attendant female figure who is conventionally outside the prison. The poem moves to re-establish a 'normal' placing of female and male, rather than to liberate the prisoner into human society. Yet 'On a Political Prisoner' should not be mistaken for sentimental male chauvinism: the landscape to which the prisoner is finally assimilated has all the astringent isolation one could wish for in a poem by Yeats.

Con Markievicz had not seen the last of prison when the Treaty with Britain was signed. In the course of the Civil War, both she and Maud Gonne Mac Bride were jailed by the new Irish government they had done so much to make possible. Yeats intervened on behalf of the latter but, according to his first biographer, he told the authorities that it would not do Madame Markievicz 'any harm' to be kept in prison. To a degree, the story indicates the relative comfort a woman of her class enjoyed in an Irish prison, but it also signals the poet's willingness to accept the imprisonment of associates with equanimity. Astringent isolation doubtless faciliated this acceptance.

*

We do not lack accounts of Yeats's subsequent political development. If Conor Cruise O'Brien's seminal essay 'Passion and Cunning' (1965) has been much responded to (notably by Patrick Cosgrave, Grattan Freyer, and Elizabeth Cullingford), the central fact of the poet's deep interest in, and occasional express admiration of, fascist policy remains unshaken, even in Dr. O'Brien's own quietly revised version of his essay (1988). Mussolini's imprisonment of intellectuals and political opponents is now best known through the case of Antonio Gramsci, whose *Prison Diaries* (1929-1935) continues to exercise a powerful influence in Marxist theories of culture. The advent to power of Adolf Hitler inaugurated a far more drastic extension of imprisonment as a form of political warfare against specific individuals. An examination of Yeats's response to an appeal on behalf of one of Hitler's prisoners can serve to illustrate how the poet had pushed beyond the 'no harm' attitude to Markievicz, and further to illustrate the obligation placed on critics to report such changes of attitude fully and accurately. Attention to the fate of one prisoner, or the failure to attend to one prisoner, has implications for each and every prisoner similarly placed. The case history which briefly follows is thus exemplary rather than exclusive.

The prisoner in question, Karl von Ossietsky, had been born on 3 October 1889 to an impoverished Silesian petty aristocratic family. His father had worked as a clerk in a Hamburg lawyer's office, and the family had never been landed, consisting instead in a succession of officers, clergy, and minor officials. As a young man Ossietsky was influenced by the monism of Ernst Haechel, and the social democratic politics of August Bebel. In 1913 he married an Englishwoman, Maud Hester Lichfield Woods. During the First World War, he published a number of articles later collected under the title, *The Advance of the New Reformation* (1919). By now, he had moved to Berlin where he became secretary of the German Peace Society from which he seceded to form the Peace League of War Veterans. Ossietsky had been in trouble with the authorities as early as 1913, and as a journalist he developed an uncompromising style in attacking German militarism under the Kaiser, during the Weimar period, and after. Essentially, he was a pacifist with distinct liberal commitments politically. But as the Nazis came closer and closer to achieving power, he broke from the sectarian position of many German liberals and socialists to recommend a comprehensive alliance with the Communists against Hitler. In November 1931 Ossietsky was tried for treason in connection with an article published in *Die Weltbuhne* two years earlier. (His journal, which brought politics and cultural commentary together, had published several articles on James Joyce between 1927 and 1932.) Sentenced to eighteen months, he entered prison on 10 May 1932, but was released under an amnesty declared at Christmas. On 30 January 1933 Hitler was elected Chancellor, and on 27 February 1933 Ossietsky was re-arrested and held in Spandau Prison in Berlin. From there he was transferred to Sonnenburg, by now converted into a concentration camp. The following year he was moved yet again, this time to Papenburg-Esterwegen in the boggy north-western region of Germany.

Imprisonment here was for Irish observers (such as there were) incomparable in an absolute sense. Ossietsky's position was different from that of a Con Markievicz or a Maud Gonne. It was wholly unlike that of Scawen Blunt fooling around in Galway Jail. It was fearful. The rights of a prisoner of the Nazis scarcely existed: in their camps he was unlikely to be visited by daughters of his authors, for the relation of the prison to the milieu of the intellectual no longer distinguished between a publisher and his author, as in the enlightened days of Joseph Johnson and the Edgeworths. Ironically, as Europe stamped on the last vestiges of Enlightenment, Ireland's leading intellectual stood by the Enlightenment principle of an individual's right not to be conscripted to any cause, however good. But this is to anticipate Yeats's reaction.

Even now, Ossietsky was not wholly forgotten, being visited (with great difficulty) by a Swiss Red Cross official, Carl J. Burckhardt, who described the pacifist/journalist as: 'A shaking, deadly pale something, a being which appears to have lost all feeling, one eye swollen, his teeth apparently smashed, dragging a broken and badly mended leg.'

About the time of Ossietsky's transfer, an exiled newspaperman gave Thomas Mann a 'shattering' account of conditions in these camps. In his diary for 13 February 1934, Mann recorded 'the abject condition of a man who was released from a concentration camp'. He continued:

Mute, frozen, a film over his eyes, unable to communicate: endlessly, crazily apologizing. People who have been to visit the pacifist Ossietzky claim he is insensible to anything said to him or asked of him, but simply marches in goose-step around the room, saluting and shouting 'Yes, sir!' The world knows what is going on, but in its moral obtuseness and helplessness it suppresses any indignation and would cooly refuse to be moved by any appeal.

International concern for the prisoner's fate had been mobilised in January 1934, when Wickham Steed published a letter in the London *Times*. In June of that year a campaign to have the Nobel Peace Prize awarded to Ossietsky was launched with the objective of getting him out of Germany, a campaign which was to draw the support of Albert Einstein, Aldous Huxley, Romain Rolland and Virginia Woolf, amongst others.

The approach to Yeats was badly handled, without doubt, and was attempted by unlikely emissaries. Admittedly Ethel Mannin, the novelist who described herself as a socialist and a materialist, had become quite intimate with Yeats. Ernst Toller, on the other hand, lay beyond Yeats's usual horizons: Jewish by birth, an expressionist in his drama, both left-wing and pacifist in his politics, he had been imprisoned in 1919 for five years. The two met one evening at a party in the Soviet Embassy in London, where they drank a good deal of vodka. Hearing that Mannin was due to dine with Yeats, Toller impulsively decided that this was the opportunity to state Ossietsky's case. Fortified with more vodka, they went by taxi to meet Yeats at the Savile Club and proceeded on foot to Claridge's Hotel. In these surroundings, the prisoner's case was made. In *Privileged Spectator*, Mannin provides a detailed account of what happened:

> Over the drinks – I believe Toller and I continued with vodka – I explained to the non-political Yeats about Ossietsky. Toller followed up eagerly with the importance of Ossietsky securing the Nobel Peace Prize, and how it was necessary to find immediately someone who was already a Nobel prize winner to support this movement.
>
> I knew before Toller had finished that Yeats would refuse. He was acutely uncomfortable about it, but he refused. He never meddled in political matters, he said; he never had. At the urging of Maud Gonne he had signed the petition on behalf of Roger Casement, but that was all, and the Casement case was after all an Irish affair. He was a poet, and Irish, and had no interest in European political squabbles. His interest was Ireland, and Ireland had nothing to do with Europe politically; it was outside, apart. He was sorry, but this had always been his attitude.
>
> Toller and I looked at each other. Toller's eyes filled with tears. Perhaps, he said, with emotion, perhaps one felt differently about these things if one had been in prison oneself . . . Toller and I pleaded alternately, that Ossietsky was not a political person, merely a liberal writer suffering as so many liberal writers and artists had suffered and were suffering under the Nazi regime; that it might be the saving of Ossietsky's life if he were granted this prize.
>
> Yeats no less stubbornly persisted that he knew nothing about Ossietsky as a writer; that he could not be involved in a matter of this kind; that it was no part of an artist's business to become involved in affairs of this kind. He was sorry. He was very sorry.
>
> His distress was obvious; he was genuinely troubled that there had been made to him this request which he could not fulfil.

Badly handled or not, by persons drunk or sober, the exchange with Yeats is highly revealing of his altered attitude to the potent issue of the intellectual and imprisonment. Yeats had admired Toller as a dramatist in a letter to Mannin of 4 March [1935?]. It is doubtful he did not know that Toller's verse play *The Swallow Book* (1924), was based on the experience (not unlike Constance Markievicz's) of being visited in his prison cell by a bird, a swallow in Toller's case. The play after all was translated into English twice. The German dramatist may have touched a raw nerve in distinguishing between writers who had, and writers who had not, some first-hand knowledge of jails. And Mannin was less than accurate in describing the prisoner as 'not a political person'. But two points in relation to Yeats himself are inescapable – the disingenuous nature of his defence, and his distress in making such a defence.

It is not necessary to cite the abundant evidence of Yeats's active interest in European affairs both before and after the consultation in Claridge's. He read the newspapers, and he travelled frequently to Italy, Spain, and France. From the private domain his friend and biographer, Joseph Hone, reports that the poet was much impressed by German legislation of September 1933, in Yeats's words 'a new law in that country whereby ancient and impoverished families can recover their hereditary properties'. (Less grandly, the Nazis required proof of 'Aryan' ancestry dating back to 1760, a mechanism for dispossessing Jewish landowners.) Yeats – Hone added – read many popular books on Nazi Germany but none of these seems to have impressed him with any sense of urgency in getting a prisoner out of Germany. In the public domain 'A General Introduction for my Work' (1937) is sufficiently indulgent towards hatred, violence and strong minds in Europe to leave one in little doubt as to the particular chancelleries in which the Introduction was most appreciated.

Yet it is worth bringing together some details of Yeats's attitude and behaviour in relation to Ossietsky's captors. His approval of the 1933 laws on 'hereditary' property has already been noted. In 1934 he accepted the Goethe Plakette, awarded by the lord mayor of Frankfurt. In 1936 he rebuffed Toller and Mannin in the manner described by the latter. Yeats's subsequent letter of self-justification to Mannin, written *c.* 8 May 1936, offers a defence of his conduct equally bankrupt on the intellectual and moral accounts:

If the Nobel Society did what you want, it would seem to the majority of the German people that the Society hated their Government for its politics, not because it was inhuman – that is the way their newspapers would explain it. What victims of the Russian Government had been given the peace prize and so on? If Germans are like my own countrymen the antagonism so roused would doom the prisoner you want to help, either to death or to long imprisonment.

In effect, Ossietsky was a hostage either to the Nazis' journalistic standards or to the Irish-like vindictiveness of his jailers!

This was not all. In August 1938, on the day after Germany mobilised for the invasion of Czechoslovakia, Yeats published an interview in the *Irish Independent* (of all papers!) publicly reiterating his approval of Nazi legislation on race and property, and giving a European context to the explicitly Irish material of his play 'Purgatory'. (The choice of newspaper is a measure of Yeats's insistence in propagating his views to the Irish public at large, for the *Independent* was an old adversary of his, the organ of middle-class Catholic public opinion.) Finally, in the following month (the month of Chamberlain's Munich agreement), Yeats accepted a presentation copy of *Germany Speaks*, a collection of twenty-one propagandist essays by 'leading members of party and state with a preface by Joachim von Ribbentrop'. Among discussions of Nazi agriculture and sport, there is a lengthy account of 'The Act for the Prevention of Hereditary Diseased Offspring' and the provision (of 28 June 1935) abolishing 'the maxim according to which no offence can be punished unless it is specifically mentioned in the existing code' of law. To be sure, the book was planted on Yeats by a wily diplomat anxious (like, and so unlike, Ernst Toller) to have a Nobel prize winner on his side. But as the inscription makes clear, *Germany Speaks* did not arrive unsolicited through the post: 'Eduard Hempel, German Minister to Ireland gave this book to W. B. Yeats in remembrance of an unforgettable afternoon he spent with him in September 1938.'

Before the last year of peace was ended, Yeats received another complimentary copy, of Mannin's *Privileged Spectator* with its account of the Claridge's Hotel episode. Though Ossietsky was seven months dead (4 May 1938), though Germany had by now occupied the Sudetenland, though Bene's government had fallen in

Czechoslovakia, and (8-14 November) virulent anti-Semitic pogroms had occurred in Germany, the poet's response in relation to the once admired German-Jewish dramatist was 'Damn Toller.' Toller obliged by committing suicide on 5 May 1939. When Yeats died in January 1939, the German Foreign Office sent its condolences.

On the rare occasions when the charge of fascism is raised against Yeats, there would appear to be some tampering with the evidence by the self-appointed defence, or at best these advocates have been more than a little forgetful of detail. The presentation copy is nowhere mentioned, though it is preserved in the National Library of Ireland. And the incident of the prisoner in 1935/6 is minimised by various means. One critic forgets Ossietsky's Christian name, another mistakenly claims that he was Jewish, a third claims that he was a poet, a fourth that the Nobel Prize for *Literature* was sought. Of particular concern here is the very minor degree of importance vested in the dilemma of the prisoner, and in the responsibility of the intellectual towards the prisoner of a vile and brutal regime. To forget a prisoner's name is an act of aggression. To suspend a prisoner's life from the balance of press freedom and press corruption within that tyranny is a cynical act of betrayal.

*

Ireland, and Irish culture, were not so hermetically separate from Europe as Yeats liked to argue when defending himself to his left-wing admirer. In the 1930s, other perspectives on racist tyranny and oppression were available. There is a painting by Jack Yeats, 'Tinkers' Encampment: The Blood of Abel' (1940), which has been accepted as an allegorical vision of Europe at war, the Europe of those dictators for whom tinkers (like Jews, blacks, and other 'non-Aryans') were mere fuel. Jack Yeats's style had changed profoundly during the intervening years: the strongly-framed elements of earlier pictures were now apprehended in a solving moment (or dissolving) of vision. Tributes to his artistic vision by Thomas MacGreevey, Samuel Beckett, and John Berger acknowledge in different ways the political significance of the work, frequently singling out the 1940 painting. The present writer can record that Bertie Anderson (the hermit of Ballisodare and a friend of the painter's) spoke at some length in the summer of 1967 about Jack Yeats's active support for the Irish republican cause in the 1920s, providing money and shelter, and his life-long disapproval of W. B. Yeats right-wing stance. 'Communicating with Prisoners' answers 'On a Political Prisoner', not least in its high-populist portrayal of women in their (tricolour beribboned?) hats and its emphasis on the plural scale of imprisonment. 'The Blood of Abel', painted in the year after the poet's death, takes this its half-title from the origin tale of fraternal disagreement, not perhaps without a degree of grief – a sister had also died – but with a larger reference to the war for which (quoting his beloved John Mitchel) W. B. Yeats had prayed.

However, Yeats the poet did not differ simply with his brother the painter. There is a less resonant tradition in which literature and politics engage in dialogue, a less dictatorial one than the Yeatsian. Joyce is perhaps its founder, but Samuel Beckett unquestionably exemplifies it. The translations for Nancy Cunard's *Negro Anthology* (1935) logically preface his decision to stay in Paris when the Germans invaded, to assist the Resistance in whatever way he could. Beckett's fiction is of course transformed by the war. Whereas the 1930s stories are articulate to a fault, from *Watt* onwards the prose, in a decisive manner, is less masterly. Alec Reid has underlined this artistic humility in the face of barbaric might in the quoting title of his memoir of Beckett – *All I Can Manage, More than I Could*: there one reads of the writer's response to Nazism, 'I couldn't stand with my arms folded.' Two further details – one of them more than a detail – sustain Beckett's relevance to the question of communicating with prisoners. One simply is Reid's account of his friend rescuing Brendan Behan from police detention in Paris. The other involves the whole question of the aesthetic relation to brutal imprisonment, a question inscribed in Irish critical debate in the strangeness of names.

Theodor Adorno singled out Beckett's *Endgame* (1958) as an exceptional work of art which remained true to the actuality of the War in that it attempted no reproduction, representation, or communication of the War's specific components. At the heart of Adorno's essay is a speculation that, behind the play, there is

> something like an apoplectic middle-aged man taking his midday nap, a cloth over his eyes. . . . This image . . . becomes a sign only after one has become aware of the face's loss of identity, and aware

also of the repulsive nature of that physical concern which reduces the man to his body and places him already among the corpses. Beckett focusses on such aspects until that family routine from which they stem pales into irrelevance.

In *Dialectic of Enlightenment*, Adorno and Max Horkheimer had earlier used similar terms to characterise philosophically the victim of brutal imprisonment. Likewise, they spoke of 'the strong-armed man who stands up whenever someone fears him', a figure all but discernible in *Waiting for Godot*. In other words, Beckett's drama provides a means to interrogate interrogation. Without limiting the results to confession false or otherwise, art may question the dreadful collapse of Enlightenment into barbarism, a collapse emblemised in the figure of the prisoner enmeshed in that sadistic parody of human community and human individuality which is imprisonment. In Beckett's work (Adorno suggests) we discover anticipatory and retrospective powers. The coercive family, the fascist cellar, post-nuclear desolation – none of these mutual quotients of a new extreme domination is excluded from the play.

It may seem that one is far removed from the actual condition of a seventy-year-old prisoner in Poldsmoor Prison. Yet thought like Adorno's helps us to remember more than the solitary prisoner. His intractable prose makes no concession in demonstrating the secret collusions by which we perpetuate the shackles we deplore. By similar means might we not come to an understanding of W. B. Yeats's hyperstatic fear of the crowd, the mob, the people mobile; or seek an explanation why nothing like *Die Weltbuhne* has scrutinised Irish culture, violence in Ireland? For, if Yeats is unquestionably a great poet, what is the nature of his great fear? And what is it about great art which can tolerate the intolerable? These difficult inquiries lie in the future, and their pathology might include the mechanism whereby critics, who venerate the integrity of the individual and deplore moralising, nevertheless succeed too often in speaking only good of the immortals. In contrast, a sentence of Adorno's, like a play of Beckett's, makes demands, and demands an end to considerate amnesia.

Nelson Mandela reverses the categories, or at least their relations, in a way which should command the writer's most respectful attention. His courage exists in inverse proportion to his writings. He has not chosen to publish a prison journal smuggled out (as his comrade Govan Mbeki's was) on bits of toilet paper. And this decision being a choice, it acts for those who have patiently waited at the gates as a omen of emancipation. He is alive because his name has not been forgotten, nor his faith travestied, his objective compromised, bargained for or surrendered. He has endured in a world of ever-increasing manipulative resourcefulness: in which junk literature and the golden opinions of forget-me-do critics – criticism without critique – swamps all reflection. He has succeeded in renewing the bond between prisoner and reader in an age when 'communication theory' has threatened to isolate one as much the other. And one secondary reason for his triumph in endurance might be recognised in the willingness of a few obscure figures to think hardly about the art, criticism, and politics of a shameless culture.

NOTES ON CONTRIBUTORS

CHINUA ACHEBE: Born in 1930 in eastern Nigeria; his first novel, *Things Fall Apart* (Heinemann 1958), has sold over three million copies and has been translated into many languages; his latest novel is *Anthills of the Savannah* (Heinemann 1987). In 1987 Achebe was granted his country's highest accolade for intellectual distinction, the Nigerian National Merit Award.

JOHN BANVILLE: Commenced publishing fiction with *Long Lankin* (Secker 1970); his most recent novel is *Mephisto* (Secker 1987); appointed literary editor of *The Irish Times* in 1988.

SAMUEL BECKETT: Has lived in Paris since the 1930s; Ireland's most distinguished novelist and playwright, he was awarded the Nobel Prize for Literature in 1969.

MARY BENSON: Born in Pretoria, South Africa, political writer, playwright, and novelist; her standard biography of Nelson Mandela is currently available in Penguin Books.

EDWARD BOND: The spear-head of political drama in England today; his recent *Poems 1978-1985* was published by Methuen in 1987.

HUBERT BUTLER: Born in 1900 in Kilkenny; traveller and essayist; the second volume, *The Children of Drancy*, of his collected writings was published by The Lilliput Press in 1988.

DARDIS CLARKE: Technical writer in the construction industry.

NEIL CORNWELL: Born 1942; has taught Russian literature at the New University, of Ulster, Queen's University, Belfast, and the University of Bristol. Collaborated with Hugh Maxton in translating Josef Brodsky's 'Great Elegy for John Donne'.

PATRICK GALVIN: Born Cork 1927, poet and playwright, a member of Aosdána.

GUNTER GRASS: The outstanding German novelist of the post-war era, his *The Meeting at Telgte* (English translation published by Secker in 1979) is of particular relevance to the Irish condition.

SEAMUS HEANEY: In 1986 he delivered the T. S. Eliot Memorial Lectures which have been published (with other critical essays) as *The Government of the Tongue* (Faber 1988).

DESMOND HOGAN: His latest publication is *Lebanon Lodge* (Faber 1988), a collection of short stories.

BENEDICT KIELY: Born in County Tyrone in 1919, a prolific novelist, short-story writer and broadcaster; member of the Irish Academy of Letters and of Aosdána.

THOMAS KINSELLA: Poet and translator, born in Dublin in 1929; in recent years his poetry has been made available through the 'Peppercanister' series, the most recent being *Out of Ireland* and *St Catherine's Clock* (both 1987); the senior figure in Irish poetry today.

MICHAEL LONGLEY: The most distinguished poet living in Northern Ireland today; his *Poems 1963-1983* was issued as a King Penguin in 1986.

W. J. MC CORMACK: Literary historian, and secretary of the Irish Writers' Union. The Lilliput Press issued his *The Battle of the Books: Two Decades of Irish Cultural Debate* in 1986.

MEDBH MC GUCKIAN: Born in Belfast in 1950; her work is published by Oxford University Press; she has recently been writer-in-residence at Queen's University, Belfast.

DEREK MAHON: Born Belfast 1941, educated Trinity College, Dublin; has extended his work as one of the finest poets of his generation through translation (mainly from French) and adaptation of fiction to television.

HUGH MAXTON: His volume of translations, *Between; Selected Poems of Agnes Nemes Nagy*, is jointly published by Corvina Press of Budapest and Dedalus Press of Dublin; a collection of original poems and prose-poems, *The Puzzle Tree Ascendant*, appears under the Dedalus imprint (1988).

AOIBHEANN MULLAN: Professional translator (German-Italian); a graduate of University College Dublin, now living in Derry.

RICHARD MURPHY: Born County Mayo 1927, spent part of his childhood in Ceylon (now Sri Lanka), educated at Oxford and the Sorbonne; his latest collection of poems is *The Price of Stone* (Faber 1985).

AGNES NEMES NAGY: Born 1922, active in the resistance to fascism during the war but silenced at the end of the 1940s; a dominant figure in contemporary Hungarian writing, she was awarded the Kossuth Prize in 1983.

KEVIN O'DONNELL: Prize-winning composer (Macaulay Fellowship, 1986, etc.), his *String Trio* inaugurated the Derry Season of Musical Events in 1987.

MORGANE WALLY SEROTE: Since 1986 he has lived in London where he now works full-time for the ANC's Department of Art and Culture; his most recent publication is *A Tough Tale* (1987).